Auguste Rodin
in the Albertinum

ASTRID NIELSEN

Auguste Rodin
in the Albertinum

Staatliche Kunstsammlungen Dresden | Albertinum

Sandstein Verlag

*"… I am very pleased to be so well represented in your Museum,
all the more so by several plasters rather than by a single marble …"*[1]

Auguste Rodin in Dresden

ASTRID NIELSEN

Auguste Rodin influenced the sculpture of an entire century in a way that can well be compared with the impact of Michelangelo on the art of the High Renaissance.[2] Until he was 40 years old, however, he won little recognition for his art. The turning point towards world fame and success did not occur until 1880, when he was awarded the state commission for the "Gates of Hell", inspired by Dante's "Divine Comedy", which he designed as the portal for a new Museum of Decorative Arts in Paris. Many of Rodin's sculptures were developed out of this major project, which he continued to work on throughout his life. In addition, he produced individual figures, portraits, monuments and drawings. The sculptor also had a keen interest in the new medium of photography and used it to bring his works to the attention of a broader public and as an aid to interpretation. Through his collaboration with the photographer Eugène Druet, beginning in 1896, numerous photographs were produced showing Rodin's works from unusual perspectives and in an atmospheric setting.

The Dresden Skulpturensammlung was the first German museum to purchase works by the sculptor. This

left
Unknown photographer:
Albertinum – cast collection,
Olympia Hall

right
Eugène Druet: Auguste Rodin
in his studio in Meudon. 1902

was thanks to the Director at the time, Georg Treu (1843–1921). By the time the last work was purchased in 1912, the Museum owned a total of 20 works, thus boasting the largest Rodin collection in Germany – and perhaps also the most unusual, since the collection not only includes bronzes and one marble sculpture but consists primarily of works sculpted in plaster. Furthermore, the renowned museum director also purchased photographs by Eugène Druet because he was aware of the significance of these images for the perception of Rodin's sculptures.[3]

When sculptures by Rodin were exhibited along with paintings by Ignacio Zuloagas at the Frankfurt Kunst

5

verein in 1908, the art historian Fritz Wichert made very sceptical remarks about the works. He wrote: "The Shades may perhaps bring joy to a few old friends; whether they will win new friends for the artist here is highly questionable. They repel rather than inspire." He also gave reasons why the plaster casts, as "representatives of the Rodin style in its most radical nuance" were not destined to succeed: "Some people say: 'Ah, plaster is not a proper material', while others say: 'They are casts of living people'; a third group finds them indecent, a fourth anatomically impossible, the fifth cannot accept the absent limbs, while the sixth say 'He is a charlatan!', and the seventh 'He is crazy!'"[4]

Although Wichert was ultimately convinced of the artistic quality of Rodin's work, his statements clearly show that many people reacted with incomprehension to the use of plaster as a material, because previously, in 19th-century academic sculpture, it had been used exclusively as a preparatory medium for creating a design or model. In the oeuvre of Auguste Rodin, however, plaster came to be more highly appreciated, because the artist used it to develop an innovative manner of working which enabled him to create both assemblages and fragmentations. Hence, his status as a pioneer of modern sculpture is not due only to his development of the torso as an independent work, his interest in the unfinished object, along with the associated open meanings and ambiguity, and the expression of emotions and subjectivity.[5]

Rodin also appreciated the aesthetic effect of plaster, which was fundamentally different from the supposedly more noble materials of bronze and marble. And he expressed this in his letter to Georg Treu in 1897, in which he wrote that he would prefer to be represented in the museum by several works in plaster, rather than by a single marble sculpture.[6]

On the history of the Dresden Skulpturensammlung

The Dresden Skulpturensammlung holds works dating from more than five millennia – from the civilisations of classical antiquity via all the periods of European sculpture, starting from the early Middle Ages, down to the present day. The core of the museum is the important collection of antiquities, which includes such sculptures as the "Herculaneum Women", the "Dresden Boy" and the "Dresden Zeus", as well as vases, bronzes and terracottas.[7] The Skulpturensammlung has undergone continuous development since the 16th century, its roots being in the Kunstkammer established by Elector August of Saxony in 1560.[8] The greatest period of expansion, which was effectively the establishment of a new institution, took place after 1697, during the reign of August the Strong, Elector of Saxony and King of Poland. As a result of this ruler's passion for collecting, Dresden became the first German city to acquire a large collection of antiquities on the Italian model: for this purpose, the Elector sent his art agent Baron Raymond Leplat to Rome. In 1728 he succeeded in purchasing nearly 200 antique sculptures from the estate of the aristocratic Chigi family and from the collection of Cardinal Alessandro Albani.[9] Contemporary sculpture was also collected, i.e. works of the German, French and Italian Baroque, both in marble and in bronze.[10] Between 1729 and 1747 this collection was housed in the Palace in the Großer Garten (Great Garden), and subsequently in the Japanisches Palais on the banks of the River Elbe.

When 833 plaster casts were purchased from the estate of the painter Anton Raphael Mengs in 1783, a cast collection was also established. This grew quickly and numbered approximately 5,000 objects by the middle of the 19th century.[11] After initially being exhibited in the Stable Building on the Neumarkt in Dresden, the cast collection was displayed from 1856 in the east wing of the Gallery building designed by Gottfried Semper.

The Skulpturensammlung in the Albertinum

The Albertinum has been home to the Skulpturensammlung since 1894. The Albertinum itself was originally a Renaissance building constructed between 1559 and 1563 as the arsenal of the city of Dresden. The first alterations and extensions to the arsenal building were made in the 18th century, in the course of which the facade was given a restrained Baroque appearance. After the completion of a new arsenal in Dresden in 1877, the old arsenal building was no longer required for its original purpose. In 1884 the Saxon Landtag therefore passed a resolution under which the antique sculptures and the cast collection were to be united in a new institution known from 1887 as the "Skulpturensammlung".

Hugo Engler:
Albertinum, View from the north-west.
c. 1908

This was to be housed in the former arsenal building, along with the Main State Archives. Over the next few years, up to 1889, the building was converted into a museum for the Skulpturensammlung. It took on its current appearance in Neo-Renaissance style and was named after the reigning King Albert. In 1891 the cast collection was opened on the second floor, and from 1894 the "collection of original sculptures" was displayed in the exhibition on the first floor.[12]

From this time onwards, the Skulpturensammlung was constantly expanded through the acquisition of contemporary sculptures – the Director responsible for this, who had taken office in Dresden in 1884, was the archaeologist Georg Treu. Under his directorship, the move into the Albertinum was associated with two important innovations with regard to the content of the collection. Firstly, the formerly separate collection of original sculptures from classical antiquity and the Baroque period was now merged with the collection of plaster casts, which had hitherto been allocated to the picture gallery. This was in keeping with academic and classical tradition and the ideas propagated by Johann Joachim Winckelmann in his "Thoughts on the Imitation of Greek Works in Painting and Sculpture" (1755), in which antique art was presented as a model for painters, in particular. Henceforth, the casts in the Albertinum were intended to be part of an encyclopaedic exhibition illustrating the historical development of sculpture, which would not have been possible using only the collection of original sculptures.

Approximately 2,400 casts of antique and Renaissance sculptures went on public display in a new exhibition opened in the presence of King Albert in January 1891, the works being presented in chronological sequence on the second floor of the Albertinum.[13] About 1,300 casts after modern works were installed in the atrium of the Albertinum – a structure with a skylight in the central courtyard. These casts included a major donation of models, sketches and designs by the sculptor Ernst Julius Hähnel, which he had bequeathed to the Skulpturensammlung shortly before his death, as well as the so-called "Rietschel Museum", which had been amalgamated into the Skulpturensammlung in 1889.[14] Models of the colossal fountains "Stormy Waves" and "Quiet Waters" designed by Robert Diez for Albertplatz, the models of "The Four Times of the Day" by Johannes Schilling created for the staircase leading up to the Brühl Terrace, and casts after works by such artists as Christian Daniel Rauch, Bertel Thorvaldsen and Johann Gottfried Schadow also came into the collection.

Familiarity with what was one of the largest and best quality cast collections in the world is also significant where the reception and acquisition of Auguste Rodin's works in Dresden is concerned, since it was through his experience with these objects that Georg Treu developed a particular affinity with the material and understood why Rodin held plaster in such high regard – albeit for different reasons than Treu.

For Treu, plaster casts were an obvious means of illustrating artistic styles and developments in a museum setting, and they were also easier to finance than bronzes or marble works. As regards the use and appreciation of

In the context of a picture gallery and a collection of bronzes and marble sculptures, Rodin's plasters have a very different, much more provocative impact, and they are also perceived differently as regards their content in such a location than when exhibited along with reproduction casts, as was the case in the Albertinum.[16] That even Treu was not entirely sure about the status of Rodin's sculptures in plaster is evident from the fact that he recorded all purchases of plasters in the acquisitions catalogue for casts, whereas the bust of Victor Hugo was recorded in the catalogue for original works, i.e. the inventory for sculptures made of marble, bronze and other materials.

As well as uniting the antique sculpture and cast collections to form the "Skulpturensammlung", the second major innovation brought about by Treu was the expansion of collecting activities to include contemporary art.[17] This was in contrast to Treu's predecessor, the archaeologist Hermann Hettner, who in 1877 had rejected the idea of purchasing modern works, "because modern original sculptures are not collected here at all".[18] Treu's efforts in support of contemporary art are therefore all the more spectacular, far-sighted and courageous, his aim being that Dresden should have an overview of "what is currently being done in world sculpture".[19]

sculptures in plaster, Rodin and Treu concurred, yet their approach was from two utterly different starting points. Rodin proceeded from the practical considerations of an artist's studio and a new aesthetic in which sculptures in plaster were not only an essential preparatory step for creating bronze works but also raised the question of when a work is to be considered finished, and hence whether the concept of 'finishedness' was appropriate at all. The replacement of the traditional concept of completion by the idea of sculpture as a process undoubtedly contributed towards plaster works being invested with a new value in themselves as exhibition objects.

Georg Treu, the archaeologist, had very different reasons for taking works in plaster for granted as worthy of display in a museum. For him, they were a useful resource for study and research in the field of 'Kopienkritik' (the study of Roman sculptures presumed to be copies of Greek originals) and with regard to questions about the restoration of sculptures through additions, as well as being an essential didactic medium for museum work.[15]

Georg Treu and contemporary art – the first purchases of works by Auguste Rodin in 1894

In an essay entitled "Der Pan über Dresden" published in November 1896, Alfred Lichtwark, Director of the Hamburg Kunsthalle, had described the situation in Dresden, mentioning Georg Treu and his colleagues, the Director of the Gemäldegalerie Karl Woermann, the Director of the Kupferstichkabinett Max Lehrs and the Executive Councillor in the Directorate-General of the Collections for Art and Science, Woldemar von Seidlitz. It was they, he wrote, "who had gained their reputation in the treatment of old art, but who are sympathetic to every healthy modern artistic individuality, every fresh movement, and are not afraid to defend their convictions in public [...]. These men, whose names are on everyone's lips well beyond the bounds of Dresden, are responsible not only for reorganising the time-honoured collections in rapid sequence but also for keeping them up-to-date with living art."[20] After spending the first

15 years of his term of office focusing on the fitting out and installation of the museum, from 1897 Georg Treu began to concentrate on purchasing contemporary art.[21] However, even in the 1880s he had already purchased works by the French sculptors Antoine-Louis Barye and Emmanuel Frémiet, as well as by Alexandre Charpentier and Joseph Chéret. In the year the Albertinum opened, 1894, he also purchased polychrome sculptures such as "The New Salome" by Max Klinger, the "Madonna and Child" relief by Arnold Böcklin and Peter Bruckmann, "Eve" by Artur Volkmann and "The Forest Secret" by Robert Diez.[22] These works reflect Treu's special interest in the colourful nature of antique sculpture; his research on this topic had already led to an exhibition as early as 1883. In a lecture delivered in November of the same year and published in 1884 under the title "Should we paint our statues?", he also raised the question of whether modern sculptures should return to this tradition – the result of these ideas can be seen in his many purchases of coloured statues.[23] A selection of these newly acquired works was immediately displayed in the relevant department of the Albertinum, in a relatively small room called the "Room of Recent Sculpture".[24] This also included Rodin's mask of the "Man with a Broken Nose", which Treu had purchased from Rodin in Paris in May 1894 through the mediation of Count von Rex.

In his essay entitled "Die Dresdner Skulpturensammlung", Paul Schumann reported on the spectacular innovations at the Albertinum: "Not the least of the achievements of Treu is that, as far as his resources have allowed, he has enabled justice to be done to modern art.

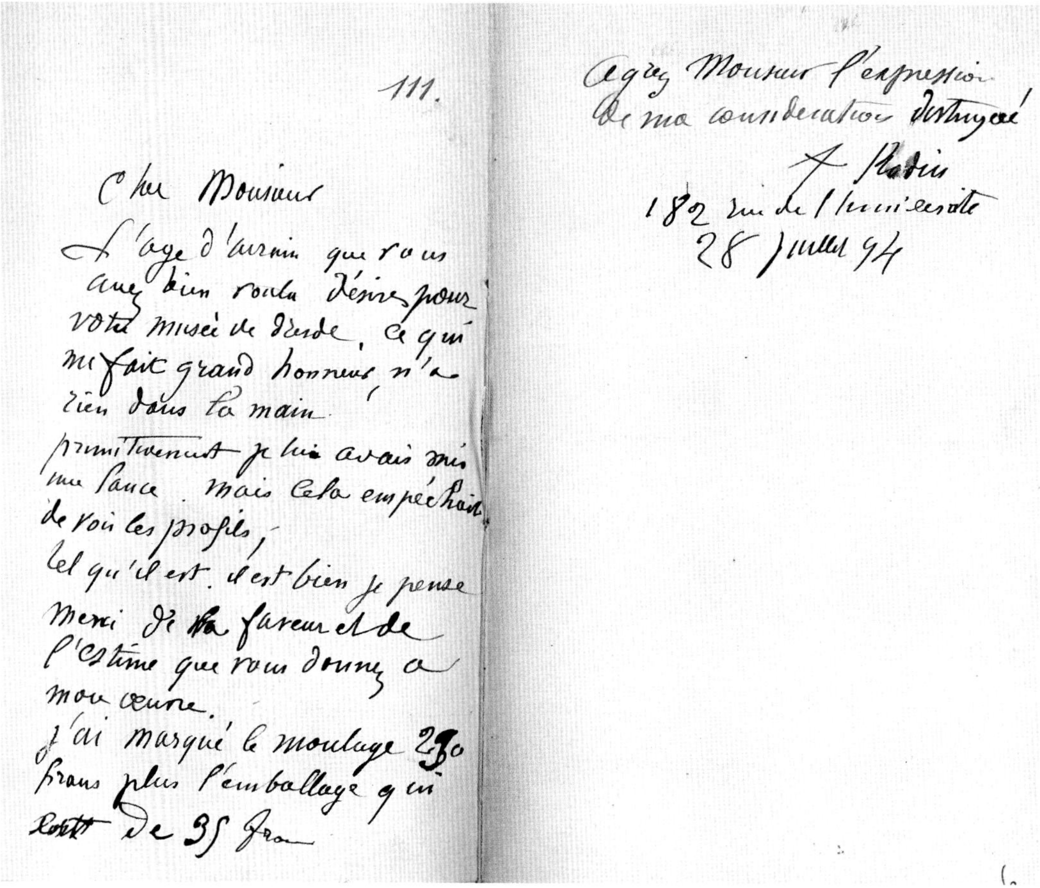

111.

Cher Monsieur

L'age d'airain que vous avez bien voulu désirer pour votre musée de Dresde, ce qui me fait grand honneur n'a rien dans la main.

primitivement je lui avais mis une lance. mais cela empêchait de voir les profils,

tel qu'il est. c'est bien je pense

Merci de la faveur et de l'estime que vous donnez a mon œuvre.

j'ai marqué le moulage 250 frans plus l'emballage qui en côut de 35 fran

Agréez Monsieur l'expression de ma considération distinguée

Rodin

182 rue de l'Université

28 Juillet 94

(.

Although the number of these more recent original sculptures is not very large, a promising start has been made and an example set that will hopefully find frequent emulation for the benefit of our artists." Schumann describes the individual works, eventually coming to Rodin: "There follows Mercury by Jean Marie Idrac (born 1849), which is highly idiosyncratic in its movement […], then in contrast to this soft and smooth figure there is "The Age of Bronze" by Auguste Rodin, a youth standing in a simple pose, with succinct and austere forms, as if limited to the absolutely necessary, with strong muscles, pronounced and well-developed, yet highly naturalistic in the treatment of the flesh. Also by Rodin is the bronze mask of an Italian man, a compelling work full of character."[25]

These two sculptures marked the start of contacts between Georg Treu and Auguste Rodin, and they were the first of the French sculptor's works to be acquired by any German museum. Treu did not initially have any personal contact with Rodin, so that these purchases were made through the mediation of Count Rudolf von Rex),[26] who was staying in Paris at the time, but that was soon to change: the correspondence between the museum director and the artist began in June 1894 and continued beyond the final purchase, that of the portrait of Gustav Mahler in 1913.[27] Previously, however, on 5 February 1894, Treu had written to Von Rex, who sent a detailed reply on 19 February, explaining the current situation on the Paris art market. He evidently paid attention to the explicit requests made to him by Treu. As well as numerous details about sculptors such as Léon Gerôme and Emmanuel Frémiet, Von Rex stated: "My next visits will be to Rodin, Falguière and Mercié."[28] On 22 March he wrote to Treu that: "In the studio of the sculptor Rodin I saw many extremely interesting works, but the only sculpture in plaster is ›L'âge d'airain‹ [The Age of Bronze], a beautiful life-size male figure. This belongs to the French state, which owns it in bronze and has also just had a copy made for a provincial museum. I saw this and believe Rodin's statement that we would probably be granted permission by the state (the Directeur des Beaux Arts, Monsieur Roujou, 3 Rue de Valois) to have a cast made. Rodin himself is of course keen to be represented in the Dresden collection, which would be an honour for him. The occasion would be favourable since he has the mould in his studio and it would probably be produced under his supervision. The price ought to be minimal. If you would like ›L'âge d'airain‹ yourself, I would be pleased to obtain verbal permission from Mr. Roujou […]. If you wish to leave things to me, I kindly request your authorisation."[29]

Treu, however, initially responded cautiously and requested some time in order to examine the photos of "The Age of Bronze" in more detail before making a decision.[30] In the end, his decision was positive, although Treu, as an archaeologist, evidently had difficulty understanding the work, since he could not explain the position of the arm; he therefore asked Rodin: "Where the posture of your figure is concerned, please write and tell me whether a lance, rod or suchlike should be held in the left hand, or whether I have misunderstood the gesture?"[31] Rodin responded, saying that he had not added a lance simply because this would have obscured the contours: "It is good as it is."[32]

The 1897 International Art Exhibition in Dresden

Opportunities to increase the holdings of contemporary sculpture were provided primarily by the International Art Exhibitions held in Dresden from 1897 onwards. These took place in the Exhibition Palace, a large complex located on the edge of the Great Garden and completed in 1896.[33] The 1st International Art Exhibition, held in 1897, gave new impetus to exhibitions in Dresden in general. The contemporary press commended the show as "undoubtedly one of the best to have been organised in Germany over the past decades".[34] The majority of

Dresden. Ausstellungspalast.

sculptures were presented in the Grand Hall of the Palace and the adjacent room. Belgian sculpture was represented by artists such as Charles van der Stappen, Paul Dubois and Jules Lagae; above all, the large number of works by Constantin Meunier attracted a great deal of attention. German and foreign artists were presented next to one another; the view of the exhibition room provides an atmospheric impression of the show.[35]

In the press it was also stressed that, "as well as the Belgians, the French sculptors are also deserving of detailed study". Most of all, they said, attention should be paid to Auguste Rodin "with his somewhat sketchy, yet fabulously life-like bust of Victor Hugo".[36] Rodin exhibited a total of six works; as well as the bust of Hugo, they included the "Inner Voice", which, along with the "Small Male Torso" was purchased by Treu immediately after the

right
Majolica portal of the "International
Art Exhibition in Dresden, 1901"

down
Sculpture Hall of the "International
Art Exhibition in Dresden, 1901"

exhibition. In preparation for this exhibition, Georg Treu
had travelled to Paris with Robert Diez, Woldemar von
Seidlitz and Gotthard Kuehl in the spring of 1896 in order
to visit Rodin and other artists.[37]

The 1901 International Art Exhibition in Dresden and the "Dresden Sculptors' Dispute"

In 1901 the next International Exhibition was held, this
time featuring as many as ten works by Rodin displayed
in "Hall 42", a smaller room adjacent to the Grand Hall,
including – as can be seen here – the large model for
"Victor Hugo", along with the "Tragic Muse" and the portrait of Puvis de Chavannes.[38] Three of the works on
show were already held by the Skulpturensammlung,
Treu having purchased them after the major Rodin exhibition during the Paris World's Fair at the Pavillon de

l'Alma in 1900: the portrait of Jean Paul Laurens in
bronze, "Eve" executed in marble and the scaled-down
bronze statue of the bearer of the key, "Jean d'Aire" from
the "Burghers of Calais".[39]

During that trip to Paris in 1900 Treu became friends
with Justus Brinckmann, the Director of the Hamburg
Museum für Kunst und Gewerbe (Museum of Arts and
Crafts), as evidenced by various letters from Treu in the
archive there.[40] As had already been the case in 1897,
the majority of sculptures were displayed in the Grand
Hall of the Exhibition Palace, which was designed by
Wilhelm Kreis. The room was dominated by the cast of
Albert Bartholomé's "Monument to the Dead". A striking
feature here is the presentation of plaster casts of the
three famous female statues from the ancient city of
Herculaneum in the elevated niches in the wall (the originals are in the Dresden antiquities collection).[41] For
Georg Treu, who supervised the selection and presentation of the sculptural works, these antique-style embel-

Ródin: Eva (Marmor) Bürger v. Calais (Bronzestatuette) u. J. P. Laurens (Bronzebüste)

136.

Adresse Télégraphique: MICHELL-KIMBEL_PARIS

TÉLÉPHONE

ADRESSES MODIFIÉES
Adresse télégraphique: MEDIUM-PARIS
LIEBER'S CODE USED
ANVERS: 2, Korte Schipperskapel Straat
DUNKERQUE: 22, Rue des Bassins
BORDEAUX: 84, Quai des Chartrons
LONDRES: 32, St Mary Axe E. C.

Transports Internationaux Maritimes & Terrestres.

MAISON MICHELL & DEPIERRE

Fondée en 1849

MICHELL & KIMBEL Succrs.

31, Place du Marché St Honoré, PARIS

FRANCO-GLOBE
AMERICAN EXPRESS

HAVRE
26, Rue des Viviers

ANVERS
132, Av. du Commerce

MARSEILLE
20, Bd Maritime

· COMMISSION · EXPÉDITIONS ·
· AFFRÈTEMENTS · ASSURANCES ·
· MAGASINAGE · RECOUVREMENTS ·
· AGENCE EN DOUANE ·
SERVICES SPÉCIAUX À PRIX RÉDUITS ·
· POUR TOUS LES POINTS DU GLOBE ·

No 588 Espon

PARIS, le 18 Decbre 1900

Monsieur Treu, Directeur du Musée Dresde

Nous avons l'honneur de vous informer que nous vous avons adressé par petite vitesse, entremise de Mr Albert Grunewald, Dresde à raison de port & emballage dûs ——— les colis dont le détail est ci-bas et qu'après bonne réception veuillez tenir à la disposition de qui de droit. Nos frais et débours ~~jusqu'à~~ Remboursement de Mr Rodin s'élèvent à francs 12 700.- dont nous vous débitons

Agréez, Monsieur, nos salutats empressés.

Beide Kisten mit den Bildwerken unversehrt empfangen am 9/1. 1901. Tr.

Pr MICHELL & KIMBEL

[signature]

DÉTAIL

Marque	Numéro	Kilo brut	Désignation
M K D	16	80	1 Caisse Eve Marbre
"	17	62	1 " Bourgeois de Calais Buste de J. P. Laurens
		142	2

Les frais de transport et d'emballage ont suivi. Monsieur Rodin nous a donné ordre de faire suivre la somme de f 12 700.- en remboursement, mais pour vous éviter les frais très onéreux qui en auraient été la conséquence, nous ne l'avons pas fait et vous prions de vouloir bien nous couvrir sans retard de ce montant dont nous nous sommes portés garants d'après votre dépêche. L'assurance contre la casse n'a pas été couverte lishments of the exhibition room were very deliberate, since they permitted contemporary art to be linked with the classical tradition.[42] The idea of creating new sculptures in the spirit of antiquity was elucidated by Georg Treu later, in his 1910 publication "Hellenische Stimmungen in der Bildhauerei von einst und jetzt" (Hellenic Moods in Sculpture Past and Present). After tracing the history of the plastic arts, he remarked by way of conclusion: "I once saw the large Sculpture Hall full of statues. As well as competent and idiosyncratic works, the vast majority being realistic images of all kinds, there were also swaggering, stilted figures of youths, and desperately writhing or lustfully rolling female bodies – and above this seething mass stood those three noble, richly apparelled women from Herculaneum genially looking down in silence at all the vain toil going on below."[43]

In his essay entitled "Die Kunst für Alle" (Art for All), published on 1 July 1901, Paul Schumann described the exhibition as follows: "The overall impression is magnificent, and anyone who wishes to keep in touch with artistic life in Germany must not miss the chance to go to Dresden this summer. […] The Grand Hall is fitted out in an extremely impressive way this time. […] Apart from a few paintings, the entire hall is filled only with sculptures. Foreign sculpture, particularly French and Belgian works, clearly overshadows German sculpture, both in terms of the number of objects and as regards the significance of the works. The Dresden exhibition has quite needlessly been reproached for that. […] The director of the Dresden Albertinum, Privy Counsellor Georg Treu, who was entrusted with responsibility for the foreign sculp-

tures, has performed his task magnificently and in doing so has simply fulfilled his obligations. He has selected the best from among the works shown in the extremely cluttered exhibition during last year's World's Fair in Paris and thus given the Dresden exhibition an incomparable appeal. Here we can only highlight a few items […]. There are ten excellent works by Auguste Rodin, the most important of the living French sculptors, including the wonderful Eve executed in marble, a plaster model of the much-discussed monument to Victor Hugo and the poignant bronze statuette of one of the Burghers of Calais."[44]

The reproach mentioned by Schumann in the above refers to a public controversy that has gone down in history as the "Dresden Sculptors' Dispute".[45] In the run-up to the 1901 Dresden International Art Exhibition a statement signed by 34 sculptors appeared in the "Dresdner Anzeiger" on 6 January, in which they complained about what they called "krankhafte Ausländerei" ('an unhealthy infatuation with everything foreign'). Their criticism was not based on artistic grounds but was simply directed against the fact that financial resources had been spent primarily on French sculpture.[46] They wrote: "The Dresden sculptors see […] with deep regret the way in which, through constant propaganda, the attention of art lovers and the general public is being directed towards foreign sculpture, which cannot be allowed to continue […]. Again and again, significant amounts are being transferred abroad for foreign art; again and again, French and Belgian sculpture is praised in the press and in public lectures, and again and again works are brought to

Dresden whose existence is due to more favourable conditions for art than are available to us at present, and which constitute a burden on domestic art, rather than being models for it."[47] Although the protest was directed against Dresden City Council, it was also a personal attack on Georg Treu. However, Treu received a great deal of support in this emotive dispute. Besides Cornelius Gurlitt and Max Klinger in Dresden, those who stood by him both personally and publicly included his colleague Justus Brinckmann, Director of the Hamburg Museum für Kunst und Gewerbe. Until mid-February, Treu corresponded with Brinckmann concerning this matter, writing on 9 February 1901: "Dear Colleague, The artists' dispute goes on and on and threatens to […] take on a more dangerous form. […] There is evidently the intention to mobilise all artists against art scholars, in particular the museum directors, and possibly to win over the Kaiser for this movement, which would probably not be very difficult, and then to replace people like you, Lichtwark, Tschudi, Seidlitz and the rest of us here […] by reliable painters or sculptors who will purchase something from their fellow artists […]. For this reason, I have asked Klinger for permission to publish a paragraph from one of his letters to me […]."[48] Finally, on 14 February 1901, Treu wrote to Brinckmann: "Dear Colleague, We have reached a cease-fire, if not peace here […]. Please also inform our friend Lichtwark about this letter […]."[49] Treu had explained and justified his actions in public in Dresden because, "It would have been a dereliction of duty for the director of our Skulpturensammlung to have

wasted this opportunity. It would have been an even greater omission if he had failed to put the great innovations, transformations and successes of French and Belgian sculpture on public display."[50]

From the outset, Treu had always sought to include works by German sculptors when purchasing contemporary art – the examples of Adolf von Hildebrand, Max Klinger and August Hudler[51] are ample evidence of this. Nevertheless, in artistic terms the outstanding role played by French and Belgian sculpture was indisputable. Treu's striving for an international perspective had begun with his first purchases of works by Rodin and continued unabated, the range of collected objects being highly diverse and intended both for the collection of original sculptures and for the cast collection. Besides the works of Rodin, the most spectacular acquisitions of French art included Albert Bartholomé's "Monument to

the Dead", which was the actual trigger for the Sculptors' Dispute.[52] The relief "The Bakers" by Alexandre Charpentier – a second version of the bas-relief in glazed brick originally installed on the Square St. Germain-des-Prés in Paris – added a further motivic element, complementing the existing works by Constantin Meunier.[53]

The purchase of the photographs by Eugène Druet in 1901

Along with the sculptures by Rodin purchased in 1901, Georg Treu also purchased a "complete collection" of photographs by Eugène Druet, comprising 273 items, 42 of which have survived in the Skulpturensammlung; the others are to be regarded as war losses. Like no other sculptor before him, Auguste Rodin collaborated with photographers because he had recognised the opportunities that the medium of photography offered for the marketing and interpretation of his works. Initially, he worked mainly with Eugène Druet, whose photographs went beyond the mere documentation of the sculptures. From 1896, photography assumed even greater importance for the artist, since in that year he began to integrate photographs of his works into exhibitions.[54] The person he entrusted with the highly responsible task of judiciously reproducing his works was the hitherto unknown amateur photographer Eugène Druet, who ran a cafe on Place de l'Alma, where Rodin often had lunch.[55] Apparently, Druet showed the sculptor photographs of his own family, as well as views of Paris and the sur-rounding area, whereupon Rodin invited him to his studio in the nearby Rue de l'Université.[56]

Druet's photographs show unconventional views of Rodin's works, but it was Rodin who selected the sculptures to be photographed, determined the viewing angle, background and form of lighting, which he desired to be as natural as possible. Nevertheless, the signatures of both the artist and photographer on the glass negatives demonstrate that the images were a collaborative endeavour.

Many of the photographs show the sculptures as works-in-progress in one of Rodin's studios – the photograph of "Eve" can be taken as an example here. The viewer's gaze is not merely directed towards the central figure; rather, the images are carefully composed to lend an atmospheric aura to its studio surroundings. The con-

the theme of the creative process, in this case not of sculpture but of photography. In Druet, Rodin had found a photographer with whom he could implement his aspirations and ideas, about which Georg Treu wrote in 1904: "This is how Rodin wishes his creations to be seen – in a light which plays with half-tones on the surface of the bodies, which dissolves shadows and coalesces forms."[57]

The 1904 Great Art Exhibition in Dresden

After the Sculptors' Dispute was resolved through Treu's conciliatory measures, Rodin was represented at the 1904 Great Art Exhibition in Dresden by 25 works, including 21 plasters, providing an exemplary cross-section through his oeuvre. Undoubtedly in preparation for the exhibition, among other things, Treu travelled to Meudon at the end of 1903 in order to visit Rodin in his house south of Paris – his article published in 1904/05 is an analytical description of what he saw there.[58]

The exhibition in Dresden gave ample space particularly to the larger plasters. They were presented in an imposing "Cupola Hall" designed by Paul Wallot, which had an open oculus like that of the Pantheon.[59] The lower edge of the dome was decorated with a frieze reminiscent of Babylonian depictions of lions. In a letter to Rodin, with which he enclosed a view of the Hall, Treu praised the décor and light effects of this room, which he considered much more effective than the presentation of Rodin's works in the exhibition at Düsseldorf, which was taking place at the same time.[60] Rodin had

sciously employed lighting separates the bright foreground from a diffuse middle ground, so that the details in the dark background are only vaguely discernible. At the same time, the tools and fragmentary objects at the edges of the image focus attention on the processual nature of Rodin's creative work. In many cases, Druet photographed only certain details, such as the half-length figures of the "Burghers of Calais" in front of a fireplace, in order to emphasise details and gestures. Sometimes the prints are enlarged, which can cause the motif to appear in a hazy blur. Druet also photographed Rodin's works outdoors and in exhibitions, such as the "Monument to Honoré de Balzac" at the Paris Salon in 1898, which is given a monumental effect due to the positioning of the camera and the angle from which it is photographed. In the Musée du Luxembourg, Druet photographed "Saint John the Baptist" from various angles without taking account of the background. This meant, for example, that the second camera was left in position and remained visible, thus drawing attention to

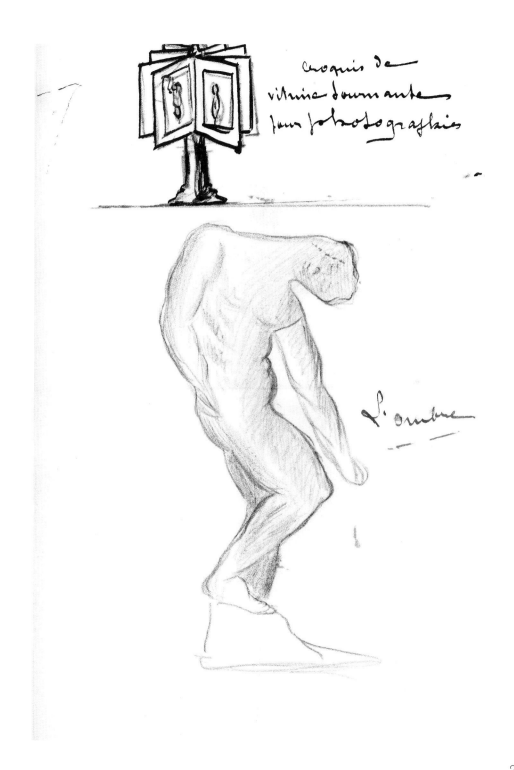

Croquis de
vitrine tournante
pour photographies

L'ombre

Grosse Kunstausstellung
Dresden 1904.

SALLE D' HONNEUR
Kuppelraum
von Paul Wallot.

also suggested showing photographs by his new photographer Jacques-Ernest Bulloz, with whom he had been working since 1903, on a rotatable frame, a sketch of which his secretary René Chéruy sent to Georg Treu in February 1904.[61]

Although Rodin did not see the Dresden exhibition himself, he had his secretary Chéruy report to Treu as follows: "So you can tell Doctor Treu I will do as he desires. Write and say that the presentation of my things (which he had seen on the postcard) was very good, very beautiful, much more beautiful […] than in Düsseldorf, where the works were too cramped together for his taste."[62]

One of the important purchases that Treu was able to make after the exhibition was "The Thinker" in a colossal format, for which he found a private donor. Furthermore, Rodin also left some smaller plasters as gifts to the Museum – a special distinction, as the secretary René Chéruy had written to Treu.[63]

The fact that even after 1900, when Rodin was enjoying great success in Germany and almost everywhere in the world,[64] his work was still not free of controversy and his fragmentary figures often met with incomprehension, is evident from a review published in the "Dresdner Journal": "The exhibition is especially of benefit to the more than life-size figure of the 'Thinker', from the still unfinished Gates of Hell, about whose future place in the completed work we are informed by a newly exhibited photograph.

Since this figure will be positioned quite high up, the play of the muscles, which appears exaggerated when viewed close-up, will no longer stand out so much. Whether distance will suffice to make palatable the monstrous appearance of the completely broken figures of the three 'Shades', which are to be positioned above the 'Thinker' and which, in their desperation, point to the impending abyss, is something that only the future will be able to decide. […] It is dangerous to play with the End and strain the nerves of the viewers to the extent that they finally snap. An artist whose strength is in the depiction of pathological states of mind and the worst forms of decadence, including in erotic images, is not suitable to be recommended to German art lovers as enthusiastically as has repeatedly occurred here in Dresden. We need healthier and heartier bread, and we would rather leave this apostle of Baudelaire to the French, who are still healthy enough, at least at present, for the vast majority to likewise reject him, while we content ourselves with duly acknowledging his remarkable power of creating vibrant portrait busts."[65]

The presentation of Rodin's sculptures in the Albertinum down to the present day

Despite this, Treu continued purchasing works by Rodin until 1912. As a result of these, along with numerous other purchases, mainly for the cast collection, the space available in the Albertinum was no longer sufficient, and a new exhibition venue needed to be found. Thus, in the 1901 Reports from the Royal Collections it was stated that: "Of the valuable casts mentioned in the introduction, some of the most beautiful and largest have not been able to go on display in the atrium of the Albertinum owing to lack of space there. They have had to be accommodated, along with the other casts after French sculptures, in the large hall of the Cosel-Palais (the former police headquarters) in a provisional, admittedly very unsatisfactory form of exhibition."[66]

On 29 May 1902, ahead of the opening of the "new section of the Skulpturensammlung", the "Dresdner Anzeiger" published a detailed description of the rooms and the individual works. For example, the "großer Festsaal" (large ceremonial hall) of the Palace built in 1745 to the designs of Oberlandbaumeister (senior court architect) Knöffel, was to feature the "Monument aux morts" by Albert Bartholomé, Frémiet's "Saint George" and "Gorilla Carrying off a Woman", "La Jeunesse" by Jean Antoine Carlès and, on the long rear wall of the hall, "in front of the mirror, Auguste Rodin's naturalist 'Saint John the Baptist', a valuable gift from Kommerzienrat [Councillor of Commerce] Lingner".[67] Other works by Rodin were exhibited on the second side wall. Paul Schumann concludes his article enthusiastically: "And so the plaster casts after French sculptures are displayed in a satisfying way. Through their segregation it is possible to appreciate how superbly 19th-century French sculpture, which is so important for the history of sculpture in general, is represented in our Albertinum. In no other city is it possible to appreciate their achievements in anything like the way that is possible here, especially if you also include the original works that are held here – Rodin's Eve, numerous reliefs, etc. Thus, this section of the Skulpturensammlung, in particular, will have a particular attraction for art lovers from elsewhere because it is unique in Germany."[68]

At the beginning of October 1904, after his return from Düsseldorf and his visit to the exhibition there, Treu had written to Rodin in order to encourage him to visit the exhibition in Dresden and to send him a copy of his article entitled "Bei Rodin", which was the fruit of his visit to Meudon the previous year. At this time, financial constraints meant that Treu did not expect to be able to purchase any further works by Rodin, although he said he would particularly have liked to purchase the portrait of Falguières and some smaller plasters. However, he mentioned the "Thinker": "And so I am left only

AGX MORES

HOLOMÉ · DENKMAL FÜR DIE TOTEN AUF DEM FRIEDHOF PÈRE LACHAISE ZU PARIS
EIGENTUM DER STADT DRESDEN

with the Thinker. I will place it in the midst of your other works in the large hall of the Palais Cosel."[69] A photograph of the statue displayed in that location has not survived.

After Georg Treu retired in 1915, another reorganisation of the collection was planned because the Main State Archives, for which a new purpose-built archive building had been constructed in Dresden-Neustadt, were about to move out of the Albertinum.[70] The French and Belgian works were therefore moved out of the Cosel-Palais and were again exhibited in the Albertinum, although it took some time to arrange the exhibition of the French casts. Treu's successor was Paul Herrmann (Director 1915–1925). Of crucial significance during Herrmann's term of office was the restructuring of the rooms between 1920 and 1922, through which "the collection of large sculptures in the exhibition was thoroughly reorganised in two respects" and a separate "viewing and study collection" was set up.[71] As early as 1918, Herrmann reported that that year had "finally brought about the long-awaited opportunity" of making "at least a modest start in taking over the rooms formerly occupied by the Main State Archives and employing them for exhibition purposes", in order "to overcome the unbearable congestion that exists in at least some areas of the Museum and to create a less crowded exhibition, which was urgently necessary".[72] The presentation of the French casts in the collection along with works by Rodin took some time, and in 1922 and 1924 the exhibition guidebook stated that: "The casts after works by modern French sculptors are in the process of reorganisation and are currently not accessible."[73] The "Modern Sculptures" by German artists at this time were on display in the "Klinger Hall" on the first floor, the room which he had been called the "Hall of the Herculaneum Women" and had accommodated the antiquities collection when the Albertinum was first opened. This hall also housed the bronze and marble works by Rodin – the "Man with a Broken Nose", "Eve" and the portrait of "Jean Paul Laurens".[74]

When the installation of the casts had finally been completed, the "Thinker", the "Age of Bronze", "Saint John the Baptist" and "Jean d'Aire" were displayed in the

double-nave hall on the ground floor, which dated from the original arsenal building.

This form of presentation was retained throughout the following years. Owing to the "imminent danger of war", measures to safeguard the works of art had already begun in the summer of 1938, and the museum was closed in 1939.[75] Various groups of the Skulpturensammlung's holdings, such as the small-scale antiquities, were initially stored in the basement vaults and then moved to locations outside Dresden. Other parts of the collections – such as the plaster casts – remained in the Albertinum even during the Second World War. In February 1945 the building was struck by bombs and severely damaged. The stairwell on the Brühl Terrace, the roofs, the atrium in the inner courtyard and the second floor were particularly badly affected. The plaster casts

which had remained in situ owing to their size were destroyed by fire.[76] Nevertheless, the removal of the other works of art to places of safety outside the city and in the basement of the building enabled large parts of the collection to survive the war without major losses.

Ragna Enking, who took over as director of the Museum immediately after the end of the war, wrote a partly fictional but also largely authentic prose text entitled "Zwei Welten" (Two Worlds), probably soon after 1946. In this she recorded her memories of the years 1945/46 and described the removal of the works of art by the Trophy Brigades of the Red Army.[77] After visiting the various places of storage outside Dresden, Enking described the situation in the Albertinum in the summer of 1946 and what was found in the basements after the first Soviet Trophy Brigade had declared its work finished. All the works of art still in place at that time were to remain in the possession of the Art Collections, but it was found that "from the collection of modern sculpture [...] all the works by French sculptors, Rodin, Maillol, Despiau and the works of Klinger"[78] were missing. Large parts of the library and the photograph collection were also lost, but the plaster casts – including those by Rodin – remained in Dresden.

The partial reconstruction of the building went ahead very quickly so that by as early as November 1951 it was possible to open an exhibition of casts of antique sculptures in the hall on the ground floor of the Albertinum. After the confiscated works of art were returned to Dresden from the Soviet Union, starting in September 1958, an exhibition entitled "Der Menschheit bewahrt" (Pre-

served for Humanity) was opened on 8 May 1959. It presented a selection of precious objects from six collections, the Skulpturensammlung being represented primarily by the most important antique sculptures as well as Rodin's "Eve" and his portrait of "Gustav Mahler".[79] The collection's holdings were, for the most part, "depos-ited in provisional store rooms, [since] accommodating them in clearly arranged display rooms is currently not possible owing to lack of space".[80]

Over the next few years the cast collection was moved from its storeroom on the second floor into the basement vaults of the Albertinum. This was because at

Hans Joachim Mirschel:
"Saint John the Baptist" in the basement vaults
of the Albertinum. 1970s

the end of 1963 the Gemäldegalerie Neue Meister was to be installed, and so the newly restored gallery rooms would be needed for that purpose. Therefore, those works of Rodin which were part of cast collection were likewise stored in the basement until it was possible to exhibit them again in the context of the Gemäldegalerie; all the other casts remained in storage, however. The Rodin sculptures were always an integral component of the permanent exhibition in the Albertinum but were shown in different conceptual contexts.

In the course of the comprehensive restructuring, re-cataloguing and development of a newly designed presentation of the cast collection undertaken between 1998 and 2001, a large proportion of the Skulpturen-sammlung was brought back into the light of day – and where the works of Rodin were concerned, an important discovery was made: the portrait of Eugène Guillaume, which had been considered lost since 1945, turned up again, although three other works believed to be war losses are still missing.[81]

From the 1960s onwards, Rodin's sculptures were alternating components of the exhibitions at the Albertinum, and they were also shown in special exhibitions – the most important were the 1979 exhibition at the Berliner Nationalgalerie in association with the Musée Rodin curated by Claude Keisch under the title "Auguste Rodin. Plastik, Zeichnungen, Graphik" (Auguste Rodin. Sculpture, Drawings, Prints)[82] and "Vor 100 Jahren. Rodin in Deutschland" (100 Years Ago. Rodin in Germany), held in Hamburg and Dresden as a collaborative project between the Bucerius Kunst Forum, the Musée

Rodin and the Dresden Skulpturensammlung in 2006, which focused particularly on Rodin's successes in Germany during the period around 1900.[83]

At that time, the Albertinum was closed. In 2002 the situation had suddenly changed as a result of the major flood that caused severe damage in Dresden in August of that year.[84] The consequences of the flood were far-reaching and prompted a complete rethinking of the conceptual basis for the Museum. It was clear that new storerooms were needed in which the works of art would no longer be exposed to danger. What started as a disaster was soon to turn into an opportunity for the Staat-

David Brandt:
Sculpture Hall in the Albertinum.
Since 2010

liche Kunstsammlungen Dresden. In 2004 submissions were invited for an architectural competition in which designs were sought for a new central storeroom, incorporating workshops, which was to be constructed in the inner courtyard of the Albertinum. The winner of the competition was the architectural firm Volker Staab Architekten, which "conceived the new storeroom building as a kind of voluminous roof, as an elevated Noah's Ark which would be lifted forever out of reach of the flood waters".[85]

After the structural alterations, the Albertinum was reopened as a Museum of Modernity, in which the focus was to be on the period starting with Romanticism in painting and sculpture, extending from the early 19th century down to the present day. Since then, the sculptures have been presented chronologically, a basic concept which was developed, among other things, in accordance with the rooms available. The Skulpturensammlung has at its disposal the large Renaissance hall on the ground floor, where the antiquities collection was previously exhibited. Today's "Hall of Sculpture" now includes the works of Rodin, and the exhibition offers plenty of space for them to unfold their vitality and aura.

Owing to his early contact with Georg Treu, who accumulated a large collection of his works, as well as through Treu's visits to Paris and Meudon and his mediation of other contacts, Auguste Rodin had a special relationship with Dresden, which he visited in 1902 on the way to Prague.[86] During that visit Treu showed him the newly installed Department of French Casts in the Cosel-Palais and the collection in the Albertinum. In his

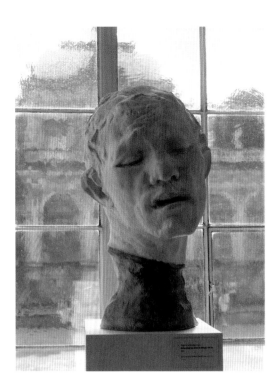

The colossal head of "Pierre de Wissant" in the exhibition "Facets of Modernity", Curved Gallery in the Zwinger. 2009

article "Bei Rodin", Treu later described the sculptor's enthusiasm upon seeing the cast of a statuette of Hypnos, of which he said that "it deserves to be elevated above even the Hermes of Praxiteles". Of Rodin's reaction to the colossal groups from the tympanum of the temple of Zeus in Olympia, Treu reported that he had said this was "the strongest artistic impression that [he] would be taking with [him] from the Dresden Albertinum".[87] That the archaeologist Treu later also successfully advised Auguste Rodin concerning his purchases of antique sculptures and objets d'art is evident from a letter that Treu sent to Paris in December 1907.[88]

When his friend Helene von Nostiz moved to Dresden in 1905, Rodin wrote to her: "I am pleased to know you are in Dresden. […] Wonderful city and wonderful flowers, magnificent museum and casts of all the masterpieces of all periods. I have a friend there in Director Treu."[89]

1 Auguste Rodin to Georg Treu, 15 February 1897, Archive of the Skulpturensammlung, Staatliche Kunstsammlungen Dresden, Artist file Rodin I, sheet 7.
2 Catherine Chevillot and Antoinette Le Normand-Romain (eds.): Rodin. Le livre du Centenaire, Exh. cat. Paris 2017; see also: http://rodin100.org/ (retrieved on 30 August 2017).
3 Concerning the life and work of Georg Treu, see: Kordelia Knoll, Georg Treus Leben und Wirken bis zum Amtsantritt seines Direktorats in Dresden 1882, in: Exh. cat. Dresden 1994, pp. 13–21.
4 Fritz Wichert, in: Frankfurter Zeitung, 9 October 1908.
5 Höcherl 2003; Wohlrab 2016.
6 The quotation in the title derives from a letter written by Rodin to Georg Treu, 15 February 1897, Archive of the Skulpturensammlung, Staatliche Kunstsammlungen Dresden, Artist file Rodin I, sheet 7.
7 At present, the antiquities collection is held in several different storerooms in the Albertinum. From 2019 it will have a new domicile in the east wing of the Semper Building next to the Zwinger, where it will again be on public display. On the history of the collection of antique sculptures see, in particular: Kordelia Knoll, Die Dresdner Sammlung im 18. Jahrhundert und ihre Entwicklung bis heute, in: Verwandelte Götter. Antike Skulpturen des Prado zu Gast in Dresden, Exh. cat. Skulpturensammlung, Staatliche Kunstsammlungen Dresden/Museo Nacional del Prado 2009, ed. Stefan F. Schröder, pp. 108–121.
8 Martina Minning, "Das Inventar der kurfürstlich-sächsischen Kunstkammer von 1587. Zur Einführung", in: Dirk Syndram, Martina Minning (eds.), Die kurfürstlich-sächsische Kunstkammer in Dresden. Das Inventar von 1587, Dresden 2010, no page ref.
9 Most recently: Saskia Wetzig, Die Albani-Antiken in Dresden, in: Il Tesoro di Antichità: Winckelmann e il Museo Capitolino nella Roma del Settecento, Exh. cat. Musei Capitolini Rom, Rome 2017 (forthcoming).
10 On this subject see: Astrid Nielsen, Zur Geschichte der Sammlung der Bronzen und barocken Bildwerke der Skulpturensammlung, in: Meisterwerke aus der Skulpturensammlung, Munich 2018 (forthcoming).

11 Moritz Kiderlen: Die Sammlung der Gipsabgüsse von Anton Raphael Mengs in Dresden, Munich 2006; On the new presentation of the Mengs cast collection since December 2016: Rolf Johannsen: Anton Raphael Mengs, Munich 2018 (forthcoming).

12 Exh. cat. Dresden 1994.

13 Kordelia Knoll, Die Einrichtung und Aufstellung der Abgußsammlung, in: Exh. cat. Dresden 1994, pp. 58–62.

14 Ibid., p. 61; On this subject see also: Gerald Heres, Das Rietschel-Museum im Palais im Großen Garten und die Übernahme seiner Bestände durch die Skulpturensammlung, in: Ernst Rietschel 1804–1861, Exh. cat., Skulpturensammlung, Staatliche Kunstsammlungen Dresden 2005, ed. Bärbel Stephan, Munich/Berlin 2005, pp. 45–48.

15 Exh. cat. Dresden 1994, pp. 58–62, pp. 131–134.

16 Nielsen/Woelk 2006, p. 49.

17 Kordelia Knoll, Die Erweiterung der Sammlung um zeitgenössische Werke und der Dresdner Bildhauerstreit von 1901, in: Exh. cat. Dresden 1994, pp. 180–185.

18 Saxon Main State Archives Dresden, Files of the Ministry of Education no. 19169: Acta, die Galerie der antiken und modernen Statuen betr. 1857–1877, fol. 223–226, quoted after: Kordelia Knoll, Die Erweiterung der Sammlung um zeitgenössische Werke und der Dresdner Bildhauerstreit von 1901, in: Exh. cat. Dresden 1994, p. 180.

19 Cornelius Gurlitt: Nochmals die Eingabe der Dresdener Bildhauer, in: Beilage zur Sächsischen Arbeiterzeitung published on 11 Jan. 1901, quoted after: Kordelia Knoll, Die Erweiterung der Sammlung um zeitgenössische Werke und der Dresdner Bildhauerstreit von 1901, in: Exh. cat. Dresden 1994, p. 180.

20 Alfred Lichtwark, Der Pan über Dresden, in: Dresdner Anzeiger no. 167 published on 16 Nov. 1896.

21 Kordelia Knoll, "Alles, was in der Kunst lebendig war, ging zu allen Zeiten eigene Wege." Georg Treu und die moderne Plastik in Dresden, in: Johann Georg Prinz von Hohenzollern/Peter-Klaus Schuster (eds.): Manet bis van Gogh. Hugo von Tschudi und der Kampf um die Moderne, Exh. cat. Nationalgalerie, Staatliche Museen zu Berlin 1996/Neue Pinakothek, Bayerische Staats-gemäldesammlungen München 1997, Munich/New York 1996, pp. 282–287.

22 Ulrich Bischoff and Moritz Woelk (eds.), Das neue Albertinum. Kunst von der Romantik bis zur Gegenwart, Altenburg 2010.

23 Georg Treu, Sollen wir unsere Statuen bemalen?, Berlin 1884.

24 Die Originalbildwerke der Königlichen Skulpturensammlung zu Dresden, Nachtrag zur zweiten Auflage des Führers durch die Königlichen Sammlungen, ed. Generaldirektion der Königlichen Sammlungen, Dresden 1895, p. 36.

25 Paul Schumann, Die Dresdner Skulpturensammlung, in: Kunst für Alle 10, 1894/95, pp. 246–249, here p. 248.

26 Rudolf von Rex was born into an old aristocratic family in Saxony, worked at the Embassy of Saxony in Munich and was based in Paris at this time. It is not known how the contact between Treu and Von Rex came into being.

27 Keisch 1998, pp. 139–144; Helene Bosecker: Georg Treu und Auguste Rodin. Eine Studie zum Briefwechsel der Jahre 1894 bis 1904, unpublished master's thesis, Institut für Kunstwissenschaft und Historische Urbanistik, Technische Universität Berlin 2015.

28 Rudolf von Rex to Georg Treu, 19 February 1894, Skulpturensammlung, Staatliche Kunstsammlungen Dresden, Artist file Frémiet, sheet 9.

29 Rudolf von Rex to Georg Treu, 22 March 1894, Archiv Skulpturensammlung, Staatliche Kunstsammlungen Dresden, Artist file Frémiet, sheet 17v.

30 Georg Treu to Rudolf von Rex (transcript), 1 April 1894, Archiv Skulpturensammlung, Staatliche Kunstsammlungen Dresden, Artist file Frémiet, sheet 18v.

31 Letter from Georg Treu to Rodin (transcript), 21 July 1894, Archiv Skulpturensammlung, Staatliche Kunstsammlungen Dresden, Artist file Rodin I, sheet 4; Keisch 1998, p. 139.

32 Letter from Rodin to Georg Treu, 28 July 1894, Archiv Skulpturensammlung, Staatliche Kunstsammlungen Dresden, Artist file Rodin I, sheet 5, 6; Keisch 1998, p. 139.

33 The Palace, designed by the architects Alfred Hauschild and Edmund Bräter, had the structure of a hall with a central glass dome. After its destruction in 1945 the ruins were removed in

1949. Today the Volkswagen Gläserne Manufaktur (Transparent Factory) is located on almost exactly the same site. A few isolated remnants of the building have remained at the site.

34 Lier 1896/97, Sp. 487 ff.; On the exhibition see: Axel Schöne, "Ohne Zweifel eine der besten" – Die Internationale Kunstausstellung 1897, in: Dresdner Hefte, 63/2000, pp. 21–28.

35 In the foreground is Rodin's marble group entitled "Fugit Amor", listed in the catalogue as "Die Woge und der Strand" (The Wave and the Beach) (Exh. cat. Dresden 1897, p. 78, cat. no. 1163). The exhibition catalogue, Paris 2001, p. 196, cat. no. 71, includes the marble version (now in Japan, Shizuoka Prefectural Museum of Art); this was originally in the collection of the Dresden businessman Oscar Schmitz, Dresden-Blasewitz. It can be assumed that Schmitz had already purchased the work at the International Art Exhibition in 1897. On Schmitz's collection see: Heike Biedermann, Einzug der Moderne – Die Sammlungen Oscar Schmitz und Adolf Rothermundt, in: Von Monet bis Mondrian. Meisterwerke der Moderne aus Dresdner Privatsammlungen der ersten Hälfte des 20. Jahrhunderts, Exh. cat. Galerie Neue Meister, Staatliche Kunstsammlungen Dresden 2006, eds. Heike Biedermann, Ulrich Bischoff, Mathias Wagner, Munich/Berlin 2006, pp. 44–60.

36 Lier 1896/97, 32, column 498.

37 Keisch 1998, p. 47.

38 On the exhibition see also: Astrid Nielsen, Clara Rilke-Westhoff und Auguste Rodin in der Dresdner Internationalen Kunstausstellung 1901, in: Blätter der Rilke-Gesellschaft, issue 29/2008: Rilkes Dresden. Das Buch der Bilder, im Auftrag der Rilke-Gesellschaft, eds. Erich Unglaub, Andrea Hübener, Frankfurt am Main/Leipzig 2008, pp. 90–104.

39 On the major Rodin exhibition in Paris see Exh. cat. Paris 2001.

40 Treu to Brinckmann, 27 Sept. 1902, Archive of the Museum für Kunst und Gewerbe Hamburg, File 1886–1960 Inländische Museen, D III, Dresden: Kupferstich-Kabinett, Münzkabinett, Historisches Museum, Ratsarchiv, Völkerkunde, Skulpturensammlung; likewise Treu to Brinckmann on 21 May 1913: "Above all, I am reminded of the Paris World's Fair in 1900, which opened up completely new vistas for me under your guidance."

41 The three statues (the so-called Large Herculaneum Woman, Inv. no. Hm 326 and the two replicas, the so-called Small Herculaneum Women, Inv. nos. Hm 327, 328) were discovered in Herculaneum in the early 18th century and were sold to Dresden in 1736 out of the collection of Prince Eugen of Savoy in Vienna by his heirs. On this subject, cf.: The Herculaneum Women and the Origins of Archaeology, Exh. cat. Los Angeles 2007.

42 Nielsen/Woelk 2006, p. 45.

43 Georg Treu, Hellenische Stimmungen in der Bildhauerei von einst und jetzt, Leipzig 1910, p. 49.

44 Paul Schumann, Internationale Kunstausstellung Dresden 1901, in: Die Kunst für Alle, 16. Jg., Heft 19, 1 July 1901, p. 443 f.

45 Exh. cat. Dresden 1994; Nielsen/Woelk 2006, p. 44.

46 Die Dresdner Ausländerei, in: Dresdner Rundschau published on 19 Jan. 1901, quoted after: Kordelia Knoll, Die Erweiterung der Sammlung um zeitgenössische Werke und der Dresdner Bildhauerstreit von 1901, in: Exh. cat. Dresden 1994, p. 181.

47 Dresdner Anzeiger, 6 Jan. 1901, quoted after: Kordelia Knoll, Die Erweiterung der Sammlung um zeitgenössische Werke und der Dresdner Bildhauerstreit von 1901, in: Exh. cat. Dresden 1994, p. 182.

48 Treu to Brinckmann, 9 Feb. 1901, Archive of the Museum für Kunst und Gewerbe Hamburg, File 1886–1960 Inländische Museen, D III, Dresden: Kupferstich-Kabinett, Münzkabinett, Historisches Museum, Ratsarchiv, Völkerkunde, Skulpturensammlung; die Stellungnahme Max Klingers, in: Dresdner Neueste Nachrichten 43, 12 Feb. 1901, see Kordelia Knoll, Die Erweiterung der Sammlung um zeitgenössische Werke und der Dresdner Bildhauerstreit von 1901, in: Exh.-cat. Dresden 1994, p. 185; On the position of Rodin in Germany, see also: Claude Keisch, Rodin im Wilhelminischen Deutschland. Seine Anhänger und Gegner in Leipzig und Berlin, in: Forschungen und Berichte der Staatlichen Museen zu Berlin, Nr. 29/30 (1990), pp. 251–301.

49 Treu to Brinckmann, 13 Feb. 1901, Archive of the Museum für Kunst und Gewerbe Hamburg, File 1886–1960 Inländische Museen, D III, Dresden: Kupferstich-Kabinett, Münzkabinett, Historisches Museum, Ratsarchiv, Völkerkunde, Skulpturensammlung.

50 Dresdner Anzeiger, 8 Jan. 1901.

51 August Hudler in Dresden. Ein Bildhauer auf dem Weg zur Moderne, Exh. cat. Skulpturensammlung, Staatliche Kunstsammlungen Dresden, eds. Astrid Nielsen, Andreas Dehmer, Dresden 2015.

52 Kordelia Knoll, Die Erweiterung der Sammlung um zeitgenössische Werke und der Dresdner Bildhauerstreit von 1901, in: Exh. cat. Dresden 1994, p. 181.

53 The relief is now on the eastern side of the Square Scipion in Paris.

54 On the earlier photographers see: Hélène Pinet, Von der Skulptur zur photographischen Darstellung. Rodins Ausstellungen und ihre photographische Dokumentation, in: Exh. cat. Hamburg/Dresden 2006, pp. 32–37, here p. 32.

55 Ibid., p. 33, note 3.

56 Anne Ganteführer, Zwischen Dokumentation und Inszenierung. Eugène Druets Sichtweise auf die Skulpturen Rodins, in: Licht und Schatten. Rodin – Photographien von Eugène Druet, Exh. cat. Georg Kolbe Museum Berlin 1994, Berlin 1994, pp. 8–21, here p. 8.

57 Treu 1904, p. 4.

58 Treu 1904.

59 Georg Treu, Rodin auf der Großen Kunstausstellung, in: Dresdner Anzeiger, 2 August 1904.

60 Transcript of letter from Treu to Rodin, 7 October 1904, Skulpturensammlung, Staatliche Kunstsammlungen Dresden, Artist file Rodin I. On this subject see also: Michael Kuhlemann, Rodin in Deutschland. Kommentiertes Verzeichnis der Ausstellungen 1883–1914, in: Exh. cat. Hamburg/Dresden 2006, pp. 158–175, here pp. 164–165.

61 René Chéruy to Georg Treu, 25 February 1904, Skulpturensammlung, Staatliche Kunstsammlungen Dresden, Artist file Rodin I – the file also includes quotations and invoices from Jacques-Ernest Bulloz. These photographs are among the war losses of the Skulpturensammlung. Keisch 1998, pp. 47, 49; Ursel Berger, Ausstellen, Sammeln, Publizieren. Zur Wirkung der Rodin-Photographien von Eugène Druet in Deutschland, in: Licht und Schatten. Rodin – Photographien von Eugène Druet, Exh.-cat. Georg Kolbe Museum Berlin 1994, Berlin 1994, pp. 22–39, here p. 25 f.

62 Chéruy to Treu, 25 October 1904. Skulpturensammlung, Staatliche Kunstsammlungen Dresden, Artist file Rodin I.

63 See p. 52.

64 Beausire 1988; Exh. cat. Hamburg/Dresden 2006.

65 H. U. Lier: Große Kunstausstellung 1904, in: Dresdner Journal, 26. und 27. Oktober 1904, Nr. 250. On this subject see also: Michael Kuhlemann, Rodin in Deutschland. Kommentiertes Verzeichnis der Ausstellungen 1883–1914, in: Exh. cat. Hamburg/Dresden 2006, pp. 158–175.

66 Report from the Royal Collections 1901, Dresden 1901, p. 1.

67 Dresdner Anzeiger, 29 May 1902: Von der königlichen Skulpturensammlung, no page ref.

68 Ibid.

69 Transcript of letter from Treu to Rodin, 7 October 1904, Archive of the Skulpturensammlung, Staatliche Kunstsammlungen Dresden, Artist file Rodin I, sheet 42v.

70 Exh. cat. Dresden 1994, p. 286.

71 Reports on the administration of the State Collections for Art and Science in Dresden for the years 1921, 1922, 1923, p. 8 f.

72 Reports on the administration of the State Collections for Art and Science in Dresden for the year 1918, p. 4 f. The reorganization concerned – apart from the works of Classical Antiquity – above all the plaster cast collection.

73 Skulpturensammlung im Albertinum (Brühlsche Terrasse). Verzeichnis der antiken Original-Bildwerke. Von Direktor Professor Dr. Paul Herrmann, Dresden 1915, Dresden 1922, p. 45.

74 Die Staatliche Skulpturensammlung. Sonderdruck aus dem Führer durch die Staatlichen Kunstsammlungen zu Dresden, hg. vom Ministerium für Volksbildung Dresden 1932, p. 21 f.

75 Gilbert Lupfer, Die Staatlichen Sammlungen für Kunst und Wissenschaft von 1918 bis 1945: Fürstenabfindung und Zweiter Weltkrieg, in: Dresdner Hefte, Sonderausgabe 2004, p. 80, note 28.

76 Martin Raumschüssel, "Die Skulpturensammlung", in: Jahrbuch der Staatliche Kunstsammlungen Dresden, 1959, pp. 89–91, here p. 89.

77 Ragna Enking, "Dresden im Mai 1945 – Ein Bericht", in: Dresdner Hefte, Sonderausgabe: Die Dresdner Kunstsammlungen in fünf Jahrhunderten, 2004, pp. 84–92; Concerning the situation following the Second World War in general see Werner Schmidt, "Die Staatlichen Kunstsammlungen Dresden nach dem Zweiten Weltkrieg", in: Dresdner Hefte, Sonderausgabe 2004: Die Dresdner Kunstsammlungen in fünf Jahrhunderten, pp. 93–112.

78 Ragna Enking, "Dresden im Mai 1945 – Ein Bericht", in: Dresdner Hefte, Sonderausgabe: Die Dresdner Kunstsammlungen in fünf Jahrhunderten, 2004, p. 91.

79 Der Menschheit bewahrt. Dresdener Kunstschätze von der Sowjetarmee im Jahre 1945 vor Zerstörung und Verderb gerettet und von der Regierung der Union der Sozialistischen Sowjetrepubliken der Regierung der Deutschen Demokratischen Republik übergeben, Exh. cat. Staatliche Kunstsammlungen Dresden 1958, Dresden 1958, p. 20.

80 Martin Raumschüssel, "Die Skulpturensammlung", in: Jahrbuch der Staatliche Kunstsammlungen Dresden, 1959, pp. 89–91, here p. 91.

81 See p. 75. On the establishment of the cast collection as a display storeroom up to the flood of 2002 and its dramatic consequences, see: Heiner Protzmann and Moritz Kiderlen, Zur Neueröffnung des Abguss-Schaudepots der Skulpturensammlung, in: Dresdener Kunstblätter 3/2000, pp. 66–76; Kordelia Knoll, Von den Anfängen bis zur Flut. Zur Geschichte der Dresdener Skulpturensammlung, in: Nach der Flut. Die Dresdener Skulpturensammlung in Berlin, Exh. cat. Skulpturensammlung, Staatliche Kunstsammlungen Dresden im Martin-Gropius-Bau Berlin 2002, Dresden 2002, pp. 27–35.

82 Exh. cat. Berlin 1979; On this subject, see also: Claude Keisch: Rodin, Klassiker einer unklassischen Zeit, in: Dresdener Kunstblätter 67/1979, pp. 162–173.

83 Exh. cat. Hamburg/Dresden 2006.

84 Gegen den Strom. Die Rettung der Dresdner Kunstschätze vor dem Hochwasser im August 2002, eds. Caroline Möhring, Johannes Schmidt für die Staatlichen Kunstsammlungen Dresden, Cologne 2002.

85 www.staab-architekten.com/index.php5?node_id=11.32&lang_id=1 (retrieved in August 2017); Dresdener Kunstblätter 4/2010: Themenhaft: Das neue Albertinum.

86 Keisch 1994, p. 223.

87 Treu 1904/05, p. 17.

88 Keisch 1979, p. 172.

89 Rodin to Helene von Nostiz, 4 February 1905, quoted after: Keisch 1979, p. 173.

Works

Man with the Broken Nose

1863/64

Rodin's earliest portraits were busts in the traditional academic style. For example, in 1860 he modelled a bust of his father Jean-Baptiste in the style of ancient Roman portraiture, and in 1863 he produced a portrait of "Pater Eymard", in whose congregation Rodin had sought refuge and comfort after the early death of his sister Maria in 1862.[1] In his portrait of a "Man with the Broken Nose" he shifted away from this tradition and set out on a completely new path. Although it is known from Rodin's own accounts that the sitter for this portrait was a casual labourer from the Paris horse market, "Monsieur Bibi", his aim was not so much to produce an individual likeness, bearing the greatest possible physiognomic resemblance. Rather, what interested Rodin was the impressive asymmetrical face, with features shaped and carved by the vagaries of life. Furthermore, the face is also reminiscent of the bust created in 1562 by Daniele da Volterra of Michelangelo Buonarroti (1475–1564) who also had a broken nose. Rodin sometimes even exhibited this work as the "Mask of Michelangelo" or simply as "Portrait M.B." – which could also stand for "Monsieur Bibi". The form of a mask was highly unusual for a portrait and was considered "unfinished", so that the plaster version of this work was rejected by the Salon – the annual Paris art exhibition – in 1865. The marble bust of the "Man with the Broken Nose" including the back of the head, which Rodin presented in 1875, was the first work by the artist to be admitted to the Salon.

Rodin later explained that the mask form had occurred by chance, since the clay model had cracked in the unheated studio during that particularly cold winter, leaving only the face section intact. The unbridled realism and dynamic surface modelling mark a turning point in 19th-century portraiture.[2] The emphasis on the fragmentary in this early work by Rodin anticipates a typical feature of his entire oeuvre and commences his celebrated series of character portraits.

In 1889 Rodin said: "That mask determined all my future work. It is the first well modelled work that I ever did. […] In fact I have never again succeeded in creating such a good sculpture as 'The Broken Nose'."[3] This portrait was purchased by the then Director of the Skulpturensammlung, Georg Treu, in 1894 and was the first acquisition of a work by this great French sculptor for any German Museum.

1 On this subject, see, for example, Ruth Butler, Rodin. The Shape of Genius, New Haven/London 1993, pp. 3–38.
2 See, for example, Schmoll gen. Eisenwerth 1983, p. 183 f.; Ursula Merkel, Das plastische Portrait im 19. und frühen 20. Jahrhundert, Diss. Heidelberg, Berlin 1995, p. 116 f.; Le Normand-Romain 2007, pp. 415–419.
3 Bartlett 1899, quoted after: Elsen 1965, p. 21.

The Age of Bronze

1877

Rodin began working on this sculpture in Brussels in 1875. After a study visit to Italy, where he saw and drew works by Donatello and Michelangelo,[1] he completed this sculpture, the first life-size figure in his oeuvre. His model was a young Belgian soldier. Rodin evidently did not wish to use a professional model trained in the expected conventional postures. He paid particularly close attention to the young man's musculature. The standing pose and the posture of the figure in "The Age of Bronze" were inspired by Michelangelo's "Dying Slave". The work was first exhibited in Brussels under the title "The Vanquished One", which explains the wound on the left temple. It then appeared at the Paris Salon in the same year, but now renamed "The Age of Bronze": "the supple slender body of a young man stretches up as if awakening from a deep sleep; […] the right arm has been raised with a jerking upward movement but has now dropped down again […]."[2] A drawing by Rodin shows that the left hand was originally intended to hold a lance.[3] After the arrival of the work in Dresden, the otherwise unaccountable position of the arm also led Georg Treu to ask Rodin whether "a lance, rod or suchlike should be held in its left hand".[4] Rodin replied that he had not added a lance because this would have obscured the contours.[5]

The extraordinary naturalism of this statue led to Rodin being accused of having cast the various body parts of the figure from a living model. It was not until 1880 that he was exonerated in an experts' report signed by several sculptors.[6]

The Dresden plaster version came into the Skulpturensammlung in 1894 through the mediation of Count Rudolf von Rex. When it arrived in Dresden it was pure white (Fig. p. 26). In the 1950s or 1960s the figure was coated with shellac in order to produce a reproduction.[7] After its restoration in 2005, the surface of the original was given its current appearance.

"The Age of Bronze" is one of the most widespread works by Rodin; there are approximately 150 versions around the world – the Dresden version is one of the earliest to have been purchased by a museum.

1 Rodin and Michelangelo. A Study in Artistic Inspiration, Exh. cat. Casa Buonarroti, Florenz 1996/Philadelphia Museum of Art, Philadelphia 1997, eds. Flavio Fergonzi, George H. Marcus, Philadelphia 1997.
2 Clemen 1905, p. 294 f.
3 Fig. in: Léon Maillard, Auguste Rodin. Statuaire, Paris 1899, Plate 3.
4 Letter from Georg Treu to Rodin (transcript), 21 July 1894, Archive of the Skulpturensammlung, Staatliche Kunstsammlungen Dresden, Artist file Rodin I (111), published in: Keisch 1998, p. 139.
5 Letter from Rodin to Georg Treu, 28 July 1894, Archive of the Skulpturensammlung, Staatliche Kunstsammlungen Dresden, Artist file Rodin I (111), published in: Keisch 1998, p. 139.
6 Le Normand-Romain 2007, p. 128.
7 Bronzed cast (Inv. ASN 1736). The mould for the cast has not been preserved. This reproduction plaster sculpture was not on offer in the "List of plaster casts for sale from the moulding shop of the State Skulpturensammlung in Dresden"; the reason for making the reproduction is not documented.

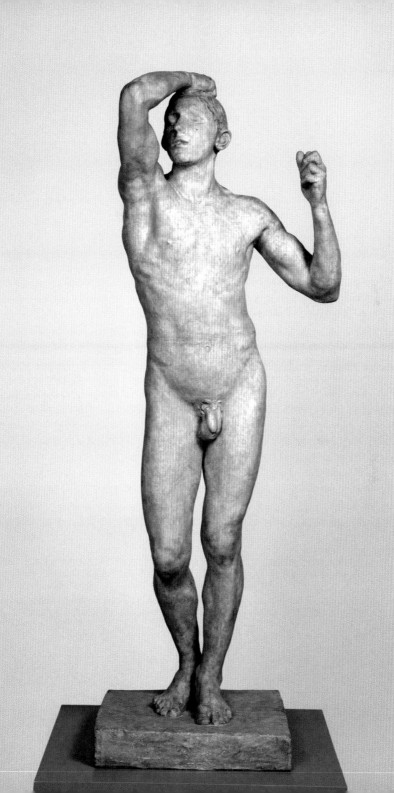

Saint John the Baptist

1878

After returning from Italy, Rodin began preparatory studies for "Saint John the Baptist". He exhibited the finished figure at the Paris Salon in 1880 – the year in which he began to experience success, among other things through being awarded the commission to produce the monumental "Gates of Hell". It was allegedly a model who inspired Rodin to create this sculpture: "One morning," he reports, "somebody knocked on the door of my studio. An Italian man entered, along with a friend who had already sat as a model for me once before. He was a 42-year-old peasant from the Abruzzi region, who had only arrived from his village the previous evening and now wished to offer himself as a model for me. As soon as I saw him, I was filled with admiration: this rough, hairy man expressed violence in his bearing, his features and his physical strength, yet also the mystical character of his race. I immediately thought of Saint John the Baptist; in other words, a man of nature, a visionary, a believer, a precursor who came to announce one greater than himself. […] All I did was copy the model that chance had sent me."[1]

The iconography of Auguste Rodin's more than life-size figure differs from all traditional representations, since the customary attributes of the cross and the lamb are absent. His "John" is a male nude captured in motion, his right arm raised with the index finger pointing upwards, and the left pointing down to the ground. The turn of the head is dynamic, the mouth open as if about to speak. The revolutionary novelty of the figure is the motif of walking, which Rodin introduced to modern sculpture through this work. In addition, it also called into question the traditional form of ponderation, i. e. the balance between weight relationships in a sculpture. Although "Saint John the Baptist" is walking, he has both feet firmly on the ground and the entire movement is shifted towards the left.

After the 1901 International Art Exhibition in Dresden this work was purchased for the Skulpturensammlung as a gift from Karl August Lingner, the art connoisseur and collector who had become wealthy as the manufacturer of the mouthwash "Odol", and who later initiated the Hygiene Museum in Dresden.[2]

1 Henri-Charles-Etienne Dujardin-Beaumetz, Entretiens avec Rodin, Paris 1913, p. 65.
2 Lingner to Treu, 7 May 1901, Archive of the Skulpturensammlung, Staatliche Kunstsammlungen Dresden, Artist file Rodin I.

Eve

c. 1881
(this marble version executed
1899/1900)

In 1880 Rodin had been awarded the commission for a monumental portal for the planned new Museum of Decorative Arts in Paris, and in connection with this he wrote to the Belgian author Camille Lemonnier: "Monsieur Turquet has commissioned me to depict the cantos of Dante in low relief and combine them in a monumental gate."[1] Rodin selected the narrative from "Hell" in Dante's "Divine Comedy", which is why the portal is referred to as the "Gates of Hell". The sculptor continued working on this project almost until his death and he never completed it – nor was the museum ever built.

Two large-format figures were intended to flank the portal on either side: the first two humans, Adam and Eve. Rodin decided to depict Eve after the Fall from Grace, with her head hanging down in shame in the curve of her arm, the second arm held protectively in front of her body and her left leg pulled slightly forward. It so happened that the young woman who was Rodin's model for this sculpture was pregnant, and so he depicted the figure in that condition: "It certainly hadn't occurred to me to take a pregnant woman as a model for depicting Eve; an accident – fortunate for me – gave her to me, and it aided the character of the figure remarkably."[2]

The posture contains references to Michelangelo's "Eve" in the Sistine Chapel, where she is depicted being expelled from the Garden of Eden, covering her face with her bent arm.[3] There are also formal similarities to works such as the "Frileuse" (1783) by Jean-Antoine Houdon or Pierre Cartellier's "Modesty" (1801).[4]

As in the case of other works, Rodin varied the size of the figure, so that as well as the life-size statue, a smaller-scale "Eve" was also created. Since this soon became one of his most popular figures, he had several copies executed in marble – more than 20 are known today. Ten of them were produced before 1900, because it was anticipated that new orders for the work would be received after Rodin's major solo exhibition in the Pavillon de l'Alma during the World's Fair in that year.[5] However, none of the marble sculptures designed by Rodin were carved by the sculptor himself. The individual works differ in certain details, such as the form of the support on the back, the hair, or the position of the fingers.

Georg Treu purchased Rodin's popular work directly at the solo exhibition in Paris for a price of 8,000 francs. It arrived in Dresden in January 1901, along with other purchases.

1 "M. Turquet m'a commandé les chants du Dante en bas relief réunis en une porte monumentale", Rodin to Lemonnier, 14 July 1880, Brussels, Musée Lemonnier, quoted after Le Normand-Romain 2010, p. 67. Edmond Turquet (1836–1914) was the State Secretary responsible for the commission, Elsen 1965, p. 15.

2 Henri-Charles-Etienne Dujardin-Beaumetz, Entretiens avec Rodin, Paris 1913, p. 64, quoted after Le Normand-Romain 2010, p. 70.

3 Rodin and Michelangelo. A Study in Artistic Inspiration, Exh. cat. Casa Buonarroti, Florenz 1996/Philadelphia Museum of Art, Philadelphia 1997, eds. Flavio Fergonzi, George H. Marcus, Philadelphia 1997, p. 130.

4 elegant //expressiv. Von Houdon bis Rodin. Französische Plastik des 19. Jahrhunderts, Exh. cat. Staatliche Kunsthalle, Karlsruhe 2007, eds. Siegmar Holsten, Nina Trauth, Heidelberg 2007, pp. 29, 88.

5 Le Normand-Romain 2010, p. 73.

Small male torso ("Torse de Giganti")

1880s

This small-scale bronze torso is connected with the figure known under the title "Giganti". The model for this work was an Italian man from Naples whose surname was "Giganti" – Rodin wrote his name and address in one of his notebooks.[1] Interestingly, this young man was sitting as a model for Camille Claudel and her friend, the English sculptor Jessie Lipscomb, at the same time.[2]

Rodin initially created a sketch-like nude study with a head and a complete right leg and cut-off left leg, which he then fragmented into a torso and separate head. The small torso displays a comparatively classical pose based on the art of antiquity: the weight of the body is clearly distributed between an engaged and a free leg, the head is turned and slightly elevated, the right arm is raised, and there is a leftward twist to the upper body. Although Rodin adopted the motif of a Late Classical torso, which he may have studied during his stay in Rome or in the antiquities collection of the Louvre, he paid particular attention to the modelling of the musculature and gave the upper body a bony appearance that makes his work clearly a product of his own era – it is far from being a mere copy. Rodin's artistic interest not only in the art of Michelangelo and the Italian Renaissance in general, as well as in Gothic cathedrals, but also in the art of classical antiquity, was reflected in the large collection of Egyptian, Greek and Roman works that the sculptor assembled from the early 1890s onwards.[3]

Perhaps it was the apparently classical motif that prompted Woldemar von Seidlitz to purchase this small sculpture for the Skulpturensammlung at the 1st International Art Exhibition in Dresden in 1897. As a bronze, and hence as a work in a different material, it also supplemented the two plaster sculptures that had already been acquired: "Inner Voice" and "Victor Hugo", which were likewise fragmented torsi.

Von Seidlitz had come to Dresden from Berlin in 1885 and was appointed Executive Councillor in the Directorate General of the Collections for Science and Art. In this capacity, he was also responsible for the administration and development of Dresden's museums.[4] Through his great interest in contemporary art, he particularly promoted the development of the Skulpturensammlung and the Kupferstich-Kabinett, and he corresponded with Auguste Rodin himself, always coordinating his actions with Georg Treu. In January 1897, in preparation for the 1st International Art Exhibition, he also travelled with Treu and Robert Diez to Paris, where they met Rodin.[5]

1 Archive of the Musée Rodin, quoted after Le Normand-Romain 2007, p. 399.
2 Le Normand-Romain 2007, p. 399.
3 Bénédicte Garnier, Rodin. Antiquity Is My Youth, Paris 2002.
4 Exh. cat. Dresden 1994, S. 292; Wolfgang Holler, Woldemar von Seidlitz – Wissenschaftler, Staatsbeamter, Sammler und Förderer der Kunst, in: Dresdner Hefte 15 (1997), Heft 49 (Sammler und Mäzene in Dresden).
5 Keisch 1994, p. 220.

Jean Paul Laurens

1882

Laurens (1838–1921) is regarded as the last great representative of French history painting in the late 19th century. He was among Rodin's circle of friends from early on, and the two artists had great respect for each other. For example, Laurens assured Rodin of his support when, following the exhibition of "The Age of Bronze" in 1877, he was accused of having cast it from a living model, and it was also thanks to Laurens' recommendation that Rodin was granted the commission for, among other things, the monument to the "Burghers of Calais". Rodin was eternally thankful to his friend for this: "[…] but I retained a deep gratitude towards this friend because he inspired me to produce one of my best works."[1]

The bust of this friend was the first in a series of character portraits which Rodin created in the 1880s and which were soon counted among his most popular works. After it was first exhibited at the Paris Salon, the portrait of Laurens was described as a "marvel of modelling"[2]. The muscles of the upper body are full of tension, as is also the sinewy neck; the head is slightly elevated in a dignified posture, the inner tension being heightened still further through the sunken cheeks and furrowed brow. The asymmetrical line of the shoulders gives a sense of agitated imbalance, with the right shoulder noticeably pushed forward. This conveys dynamism, implying a raised arm and movement of the body, which, along with the open mouth, as if the figure were about to speak, makes this portrait of Laurens resemble Rodin's rendering of "Saint John the Baptist" (1878).

This portrait illustrates how Rodin strove to capture the essence and character of his subjects. He was convinced that no other task in sculpture required such a sharp eye and such sensitivity as the portrait: "To produce a good bust you have to fight relentlessly. The main thing is not to become weak and to remain honest towards yourself."[3] Commenting on this work, Rainer Maria Rilke stated that it is "so expressive, so animated and alert" that "one cannot help feeling that nature itself has taken this work out of the sculptor's hands".[4]

After purchasing this bust in Paris in 1900, Georg Treu wrote to Rodin that he was very proud to be able to show it to the public.[5] The acquisition of this famous work by Rodin, and Georg Treu's purchasing policy, which focused strongly on French sculpture, sparked what became known as the "Dresden Sculptors' Dispute", a protest initiated by Dresden sculptors, which flared up in connection with the 2nd International Art Exhibition in 1901 (see p. 17 f.).

---

1 Gsell 1979, p. 139.
2 Paul Leroi, Salon de 1882, in: L'art. Revue hebdomadaire illustrée 8 (1882), Heft 3, p. 72 f.
3 Gsell 1979, p. 128.
4 Rilke 1920, p. 56.
5 Treu to Rodin, 11 December 1900 (transcript), Archive of the Skulpturensammlung, Staatliche Kunstsammlungen Dresden, Artist file Rodin I.

Jean d'Aire (The Man with the Key)

1886/87

The monument entitled "The Burghers of Calais", the commission for which was awarded to Rodin by the City of Calais in 1885, was erected only in 1895. It is typical of Rodin's manner of working that he removed elements from the context of this work and exhibited them as independent sculptures – examples of this are "The Inner Voice" and the bust portrait of Victor Hugo. He also presented the individual figures from "The Burghers of Calais" in exhibitions, including this large-format "Man with the Key", which was shown at the International Art Exhibition in Dresden in 1901, where it was purchased for the Skulpturensammlung.

The revolutionary conception of the monument departed from tradition in that Rodin created six figures of equal size standing side by side. The repertoire of forms for monuments in the 19th century had hitherto encompassed equestrian pieces and statues, including double statues such as Ernst Rietschel's famous monument to Schiller and Goethe in Weimar (1857). Rodin, by contrast, did not wish to honour a single individual and his memorable act, but to portray an image of civic, democratic society. In representing the six honourable men, he therefore decided against singling out a main figure and also against a main viewing angle. In an initial draft, he first had the idea of presenting the group at such a height that the silhouettes of the figures would stand out against the sky. In the end, however, he decided to do without any elevating base, so as to draw the viewer into the monument when walking around it.

The six individual figures are all barefoot, dressed in rags and have ropes around their necks. The hands and feet of the figures are enlarged, making them particularly expressive. The various gestures and facial expressions show desperation, mortal fear and tension, but also inner composure, which is manifested especially clearly in the posture of Jean d'Aire. He stands with both feet firmly on the ground, clutching the keys to the city. Rainer Maria Rilke described the man holding the key as: "… the man who would have lived for many years to come, but whose life is condensed into this sudden last hour which he can hardly bear. His lips tightly pressed together, his hands bite into the key. There is fire in his strength and it burns in his defiant bearing."[1] In 1889 the group was displayed for the first time in the exhibition entitled "Claude Monet – Auguste Rodin" at the Galerie Georges Petit in Paris.

1 Rilke 1920, p. 62. (Translation by Jessie Lemont and Hans Trausil, New York, 1919.)

Crying Danaid

c. 1889

In 1904 the "Great Art Exhibition" took place in Dresden, at which Rodin was represented by a considerable number of works. As well as large-format sculptures such as "The Thinker", "The Shade", "Pierre de Wissant without head and without hands", he also exhibited portraits and several small plaster sketches. After "The Thinker" had been purchased for 2,250 Marks, Rodin presented the Skulpturensammlung with a total of six further plasters, including several works which have been missing since 1945, including the "Crying Danaid".[1] From the correspondence conducted by Georg Treu primarily with Rodin's secretary at the time, René Chéruy, it is evident that Treu was very keen to purchase the small sketches and made several enquiries about them in Paris. Chéruy's personal response was unambiguous: "[…] For you know that he never sells plaster models except to the large museums which have insufficient financial resources but a strong artistic interest. However, M. R. [Monsieur Rodin] has never sold small objects (in plaster). – But I think that in your case, on account of your friendly and personal relationship with him, it is possible that he might give you some of his own choosing for a low price, or perhaps even as a gift, for the Albertinum."[2] In November 1904 Chéruy finally announced that Rodin really would offer the works as gifts.

The "Crying Danaid", also known as the "Crying Nymph", was described in the 1904 exhibition catalogue as a "weeping woman with her head on her knees".[3] It was designed for Rodin's multi-figure project, the "Gates of Hell" and is located on the right door panel approximately halfway up on the outer edge, where it is partly concealed by the door frame. For this major commission, Rodin designed hundreds of figures portraying a huge range of postures and movements. These included figures that were hanging down or falling, while some were crouching or crawling, and others were writhing, standing, sitting or stretching. The hunched pose of the "Crying Danaid" expresses great anguish. The title, however, does not relate to Dante. Rather, it refers to the Danaids, the fifty daughters of Danaus, the King of Libya, who were condemned to pour water into a bottomless barrel after killing their husbands on their wedding night. Thus, this small-format work by Rodin gains a new significance borrowed from Greek mythology.

Commenting on the works by Rodin in the 1904 Dresden exhibition, Paul Kühn wrote: "One hears […] something of the echo of bleakness, of the whispering tone and timid glances of loneliness. […] Shuddering in front of the sculptures, we sense the enormity of isolation. […] Wonderful figures who swallow their inscrutable suffering, sob out their pain, so that we hear them weeping and moaning."[4]

1 See List of works by Rodin in Dresden, p. 74 f.
2 Chéruy to Treu, 29 September 1904, Archive of the Skulpturensammlung, Staatliche Kunstsammlungen Dresden, Artist file Rodin I.
3 Information kindly provided by Chloé Ariot, Musée Rodin.
4 Paul Kühn, Die große Dresdner Kunstausstellung, in: Welt und Haus 13 (1904).

Pierre Puvis de Chavannes

1891

Pierre Puvis de Chavannes (1824–1898) was a member of the artistic circle around Rodin and was friends with him for many years – Rodin considered this painter his most important contemporary of all and is said to have spoken about him on his deathbed.[1] After Puvis de Chavannes succeeded, after many failed attempts, to have his work accepted at the Paris Salon in 1859, he soon received various major commissions. One of the first, conducted between 1861 and 1865, was to decorate the staircase and various rooms in the Museum of Amiens with cycles of monumental Symbolist frescoes. This was followed by commissions for large-scale murals for the Hôtel de Ville and the Panthéon in Paris.

In 1890 the museum in Amiens commissioned Rodin to create a marble bust of his friend. The sculptor first designed an initial version of this portrait, with bare shoulders and chest. However, Puvis de Chavannes was not satisfied with this heroic but, in his opinion, rather unofficial-looking depiction. At his request, Rodin added a frock coat, collar and rosette of the Legion of Honour to the plaster model shortly before it was exhibited in the 1891 Paris Salon exhibition. Puvis de Chavannes was still not entirely happy with the sculpture, because he regarded the slightly backward-leaning pose as giving him a supercilious air with a trace of contempt around the mouth, as he explained to Rodin.[2]

The surface of the bust reveals rapid and spontaneous modelling, and it is animated by small lumps of clay pressed onto it. This gives the portrait a sketch-like character, without obscuring the details that were so important to Puvis de Chavannes. The face, however, is modelled relatively smoothly and is an accurate depiction of the subject's physiognomy, as evidenced by photographs of him.

In his conversations with Paul Gsell, Rodin later recalled that, "Puvis de Chavannes did not like my bust and I have always found that distressing. He claimed I had made a caricature of him. And yet I am sure that in my sculpture I expressed all the enthusiasm and admiration I felt for him."[3]

1 Le Normand-Romain 2007, p. 621.
2 Puvis de Chavannes to Rodin, 16 May 1891, Paris, Archive of the Musée Rodin, quoted after Mattiussi 2010, p. 122.
3 Gsell 1979, p. 138.

Victor Hugo, "Heroic Bust", first version

1896

Like the "Inner Voice", the "Heroic Bust" of Victor Hugo (1802–1885) was initially created not as an individual figure but as an element in Rodin's design for a monument to the famous French writer. Rodin was awarded the commission to design the monument from the "Société des gens de lettres" in 1889, but he had already produced a portrait of the great French writer in 1883, when Hugo was 81 years of age.[1] In 1890, Rodin's first design for the monument – which was evidently based on a photograph showing Victor Hugo in exile on the island of Guernsey – was rejected by the Society. For the second design, Rodin decided to depict the poet in a seated pose, lost in contemplation, with his head resting on one hand and the other arm stretched out. The subject was nude, save for some drapery over the right thigh. Hugo was accompanied by the figures of "Meditation" ("Inner Voice") and the "Tragic Muse", as representations of the multifaceted poetic works of this literary and political writer. In 1909 the monument was set up in the garden of the Palais Royal, albeit without the Muses, and thus featuring only the figure of the poet. At the same time as the "Inner Voice" was separated from the group and turned into an independent sculpture, Rodin also cropped the monumental figure of Hugo to create the "Heroic Bust". Through the shortening of the torso above the drapery, the upper body generates a particularly dramatic impact; the cropping draws attention towards the pensively inclined head, which is no longer supported by the hand. In this bust, Rodin has condensed the vitality of the poet and the potency of his words into a sculptural statement.

This bust was exhibited at the 1st International Art Exhibition in Dresden in 1897, which proves that Rodin had already had the idea of detaching the bust from the more than life-size draft monument at an early stage.[2] The selection and presentation of the sculptures was the responsibility of Georg Treu, Director of the Skulpturensammlung, and the large exhibition was enthusiastically celebrated, the contemporary press hailing it as "undoubtedly one of the best to have been held in Germany in recent years".[3] Rodin showed a total of six works: in addition to the bust of Victor Hugo, the "Inner Voice" and the "Small Male Torso" were purchased for the Museum after the exhibition: purchases which "brought to light the most shocking aspects of Rodin's art: the fragmentary, the expressive, the improvisatory, the deliberately experimental".[4]

1 On this subject, cf. Exh. cat. Paris 2003, pp. 30–37.
2 Exh. cat, Paris 2003, p. 174.
3 Lier 1896/97, Column 498.
4 Keisch 1994, p. 220.

The Inner Voice

1896

The idea, radical at the time, of designing a female statue as a fragmented torso, may have been inspired by antique torsos such as the famous Venus of Milo in the Louvre. These influences apart, however, it is typical of Rodin's manner of working that the "Inner Voice" was not initially created as an independent figure but was derived from the scenes he designed for the monument in honour of Victor Hugo, which was commissioned by the Société des gens de lettres in 1889. In one of his designs for the monument, female figures were intended to represent the different aspects of the writer's poetry.

The contortion of the body of the "Inner Voice" and the gesture of the right arm, which the artist later removed, had initially been developed by Rodin for the figure of a condemned woman in the tympanum of the "Gates of Hell". In this small-scale condemned woman, the position of the legs and the sequence of movement generally corresponds to those of "Eve" – which Rodin designed in 1881 and had intended to complement "Adam" as a large-format figure flanking the "Gates of Hell" – but the position of the arms is different. Detached from the "Gates of Hell" as an individual sculpture, this small figure was given the title "Meditation".[1] This was then enlarged and integrated as one of the Three Muses into one of the designs for the large monument to Victor Hugo, but now without the arms. In order to be incorporated next to the seated figure of the poet, her right leg and left knee were partly cut off. The title "Inner Voice", which was then given to the work, is a reference to the cycle of poems by Hugo "Les Voix intérieures" ("The Inner Voices"), published in 1837.

From 1897 Rodin finally presented the altered figure as an individual work in exhibitions, starting in Copenhagen and Dresden, where it was already exhibited under the title "The Inner Voice".[2] The female torso stands alone, and all narrative context is blocked out in the sculpture. Vulnerable and wounded, naked and withdrawn, and yet radiating an aura of sensuality, this isolated figure is one of the pioneering works of modern sculpture, of which Rodin himself said, "I regard this plaster cast as one of my most perfect, intense works."[3] On the one hand, Georg Treu's purchase of the "Inner Voice" for the Skulpturensammlung testifies to his appreciation – as an archaeologist – of the torso and of fragmentary sculptures, while on the other it demonstrates that he grasped the radicality of Rodin's art.

1 On the genesis of this work, see Exh. cat. Marseille 1997, S. 11–37.
2 Exh. cat. Dresden 1897, p. 78, cat. no. 1166; Le Normand-Romain 2007, p. 513.
3 "Je considère que ce plâtre est une des mes œuvres les mieux finies, le plus poussées [sic]". Rodin to Prince Eugen of Sweden, 2 January 1897, Stockholm Archives, quoted after Exh. cat. Marseille 1997, p. 11.

Jean d'Aire (The Man with the Key)

1884/86 (design),
c. 1884–1899 (execution/reduced-scale cast)

Rodin created not only individual figures, portraits and countless drawings, but also numerous monuments. Among the most important of these was the "Burghers of Calais", for which he produced several designs starting in 1885, after he was awarded the commission by the City of Calais. One of the figures in this monument is the so-called Man with the Key, Jean d'Aire. The monument was intended as a tribute to the six members of the town council who, by offering to surrender and sacrifice their own lives, saved their fellow citizens from starvation when the town was under siege by the English army in 1347, during the Hundred Years War. Eustache de Saint-Pierre, Jean d'Aire, Jacques and Pierre de Wissant, Jean de Fiennes and Andrieus d'Andres presented themselves in front of the city gates, and it was only thanks to the compassion of the English Queen that the lives of these courageous men were spared.[1]

Between 1895 and 1903 Rodin employed Henri Lebossé to produce reduced-scale duplications of five out of the six figures of the "Burghers of Calais". They were reduced to one fifth of their original size and then offered for sale in large numbers – even in this small format, the figures lost nothing of their intensity. Rodin had probably been working with Lebossé since as early as 1894; in January 1903, he wrote to Rodin, "I would like to be your ideal employee."[2] Lebossé's company, which he had taken over from his father, had existed in Paris since 1865. With the aid of a machine using a similar technique to a pantograph and a procedure developed by Achille Collas, it became possible to make proportionately larger or smaller replicas of sculptures by mechanical means. The collaboration between Collas and Rodin was very close, and if Rodin did not like the quality of an executed sculpture, he rejected it.[3]

Through the production of smaller-scale sculptures, it was possible to supply a relatively large group of potential clients, and so it was not just museums that purchased Rodin's works but also private collectors. The small-format "Burghers of Calais" were extremely popular and a great many were sold during the artist's lifetime.[4] The Dresden bronze cast was purchased by Georg Treu in Paris in 1900. There, he had visited Rodin's solo exhibition in the Pavillon de l'Alma and purchased three works in all: the bronze portrait of the painter JeanPaul Laurens, the marble "Eve" and the bronze statuette of Jean d'Aire, for a total price of 12,700 francs. That year, Treu evidently had ample financial resources in order to expand the collection through the purchase of contemporary art – above all, French art. The works already held in Dresden – namely the plasters and the bronze "Man with a Broken Nose" – were now joined by a further portrait and this bronze reduction, as well as the marble sculpture of "Eve", thus also documenting the commercial aspect of Rodin's studio.[5]

1 Schmoll gen. Eisenwerth 1997, pp. 17–19.
2 Quoted after Exh. cat. Washington 1981, p. 249.
3 Exh. cat. Washington Elsen 1981, p. 254.
4 Le Norman-Romain 2007, p. 220.
5 Keisch 1994, p. 221.

Alexandre Falguière

1899

Like Rodin, albeit earlier, Falguière (1831–1900) was a pupil of Albert-Ernest Carrier-Belleuse and later studied at the École des Beaux-Arts in Paris. The large number of his sculptures and paintings, including a quadriga which formerly stood on top of the Arc de Triomphe in Paris, are evidence of Falguière's productivity. Stylistically, his oeuvre belongs to the school of French 19th-century realism. In 1882 he was appointed Professor at the École des Beaux-Arts and he was friends with Rodin.

Rodin produced this portrait of Falguière a year before the latter's death and he described his work as a "public declaration" of fondness for his professional colleague.[1] After his model for the monument to Balzac had evoked a scandal at the Salon in 1898, and the "Société des gens de lettres" had commissioned the more conventional artist, Alexandre Falguière, to execute the monument, he wished to make it clear that this decision and the subsequent controversies had not led to any discord between the two sculptors. Falguière also told Rodin that he did not share in the general contempt towards his design for the Balzac monument and proved this by producing a portrait of Rodin.[2] Many years earlier, in 1878, Falguière had already intervened in the dispute surrounding "The Age of Bronze" and was one of the sculptors who had signed the expert's report that exonerated Rodin, removing the suspicion that he had cast the individual body parts from a living model.

This plaster bust of Falguière entered the Skulpturensammlung immediately after the Great Art Exhibition in Dresden in 1904 as a gift from Rodin, following the purchase of the monumental "Thinker". It seems somewhat more restrained in its physical presence compared with the portrait of Laurens, which had been created 20 years earlier, partly due to the bust being limited to the neck and central part of the upper body. The pulled-up collar shortens the neck, which is in keeping with Rodin's own characterisation of his fellow sculptor as a "little bull".[3] The modelling is looser and freer. Rodin's idiosyncratic way of forming the eyes reveals what Rainer Maria Rilke put in a nutshell: "No observer (not even the most conceited) will be able to claim that a portrait bust by Rodin, such as that of […] Falguière […], had looked at him."[4] Rodin depicts a man who is at the end of his life and artistic career, and who appears pensive and self-absorbed, with a melancholy and musing air, seemingly at peace with himself. Furthermore, in this portrait Rodin upholds the dignity of this colleague, for whom he had great respect.

1 Gsell 1937, p. 111.
2 Cf. Arsène Alexandre, Exposition de 1900. L'OEuvre de Rodin, Paris 1900, Fig. inside cover.
3 Gsell 1979, p. 139.
4 Rainer Maria Rilke, Tagebücher aus der Frühzeit, Leipzig 1942, p. 385.

The Thinker

1903
(Colossal version; the figure
for the tympanum of the "Gates of Hell"
was created in the early 1880s,
the enlarged version in 1903)

Taking Dante's "Divine Comedy" as the basic theme, Rodin began designing the "Gates of Hell", intended as the entrance portal for a new Museum of Decorative Arts in Paris, in 1880. In the cantos of "Hell" Dante describes the world of the dead who must atone for their sins, and Rodin rendered the poet's visions in sculpture. Many of Rodin's sculptures were developed in connection with this large-scale multi-figured project. Rainer Maria Rilke, who was Rodin's secretary in Paris for a time, described the work as a "quarry of ideas".[1] Originally, "The Thinker" was created for the "Gates of Hell" as a representation of Dante, and it was intended to occupy a central position above the figural scenes of Hell; indeed, the work was originally entitled "The Poet".[2] As in other cases, Rodin exhibited the figure individually and even enlarged it to as much as three times the original size.

As regards its form, the sculpture reflects two of the most important points of reference in Rodin's art: for one thing, the posture of the "Thinker" resembles that of one of the most famous works of antiquity, the Belvedere Torso dating from the first century BCE. For another, the sculpture reveals Rodin's interest in Michelangelo and his works – the seated motif and the position of the hand against the mouth resemble Michelangelo's "Jeremiah" in the Sistine Chapel and the portrait of Lorenzo de' Medici in the Medici Chapel in Florence. There is also a clear formal similarity to the seated figure of "Ugolino" by Jean-Baptiste Carpeaux.[3]

In this figure, Rodin does not concentrate on the act of thinking; he imbues his figure with great vigour and strength, every muscle of his body being tensed, right down to his toes. In addition, the work is in the tradition of representations of melancholy as depicted since medieval times: "He is just as much a melancholy ponderer and creative spirit as a portrait of the artist left to fend for himself."[4]

Hence, "The Thinker" was ultimately identified with Rodin himself, and with his great creativity, so that today a colossal bronze version of the statue adorns the gravesite of the sculptor in Meudon.[5] This soon became one of the best-known of Rodin's works and one of the most famous in the history of modern sculpture. The plaster version in the Skulpturensammlung was purchased after the Great Art Exhibition in Dresden in 1904, financed by the Dresden banker Fritz Emil Günther. Around the world there are more than 25 colossal versions of the statue in plaster and bronze – in 1907 Edvard Munch painted the epoch-making work in "The Garden of Dr. Max Linde in Lübeck", thus creating one of the most beautiful depictions of "The Thinker".[6]

1 Rilke 1920, p. 118.
2 Le Normand-Romain 2007, p. 590.
3 Tancock 1976, p. 117; Ursel Berger, »Befreiung vom Akademismus«. Michelangelo als Vorbild für die Skulptur des 19. und 20. Jahrhunderts, in: Der Göttliche. Hommage an Michelangelo, Ausst.-Kat. Bonn 2015, München 2015, pp. 76–89, here: p. 81.
4 Melancholie. Genie und Wahnsinn in der Kunst, Exh. cat. Paris/Berlin 2005–2006, Ostfildern-Ruit 2005, pp. 463, 466.
5 Exh. cat. Berlin 1979, p. 104.
6 Exh. cat. Hamburg/Dresden 2006, p. 72. This cast of "The Thinker" is now in the Detroit Institute of Arts, the painting in the Musée Rodin, Paris.

Eugène Guillaume

1903

Guillaume (1822–1905) was a pupil of James Pradier, a member of the École des Beaux-Arts and the Académie française and later Director of the École des Beaux-Arts in Paris, as well as the French Academy in Rome. He was a rigorous representative of Neoclassicism and was one of the most renowned sculptors in France during the second half of the 19th century. In 1877 Guillaume chaired the jury that accused Rodin of having cast his sculpture "The Age of Bronze" from a living model. It can therefore be assumed that the two sculptors, whose artistic approaches were fundamentally different, were not initially on friendly terms.[1] They only developed a closer relationship shortly before Guillaume's death.

Remembering Guillaume, Rodin stated: "At first, this sculptor was far from being favourably disposed towards me. One day, when he found my mask of the "Man with the Broken Nose" in the house of a friend of mine, he actually insisted that it should be thrown on the rubbish heap! And throughout all the years […] our relationship certainly did not improve. Indeed, I had no worse enemy! But then time passed, and as you grow older there are certain comforts! For me, this was seeing that Guillaume greeted me one day and even visited me in Paris and Meudon. By that time, he had come to regard me as a great artist."[2]

Rodin's respect for the older sculptor is expressed in this poignant portrait. The modelling appears spontaneous and rapid; above all, the barely elaborated shoulder section, which reveals the rapid treatment of the clay model, is particularly sketchy, almost unfinished.[3] A few small lumps of clay remain unsmoothed on the forehead, nose and cheeks. Like the eyes in the portrait of Falguière , Guillaume's gaze seems empty, and he generally appears serious and withdrawn – a great sculptor at the end of a long, successful career. When this portrait was exhibited at the Paris Salon in 1905, it stood out on account of its "touching truthfulness".[4]

Before that, the plaster version of the bust had already been exhibited in Düsseldorf and Dresden in 1904. The portrait in Dresden is one of the works by Rodin that were given to the Skulpturensammlung by the artist immediately after the Great Art Exhibition. After 1945 the bust was regarded as a war loss.[5] During the reorganisation and re-cataloguing of the Dresden cast collection between 1999 and 2001, it was rediscovered – the other works by Rodin that have been missing since the end of the Second World War are still regarded as war losses, however.[6]

1 Le Norman-Romain 2007, p. 402.
2 Tancock 1976, p. 532.
3 Georges Grappe, Hôtel Biron. Essai de classement chronologique des oeuvres d'Auguste Rodin, Paris 1927, Kat.-Nr. 256; another version of the bust shows only a short section of the neck, cf. Le Norman-Romain 2007, p. 402.
4 Dantin, 20 May 1906, p. 4, quoted after Le Norman-Romain 2007, p. 402.
5 Exh. cat. Berlin 1979, p. 169.
6 See List of works by Rodin, p. 75.

Colossal head of Pierre de Wissant

1909

As in the case of the "Gates of Hell", Rodin also used the monument to the "Burghers of Calais" as a source for independent works which had no thematic connection with Dante or the history of the Hundred Years War. For example, he detached individual elements from the figures, such as the heads and hands, and had enlargements or reductions made of them, which he then sometimes combined in unusual assemblages. When removed from their original context, these fragments became open to completely new interpretations. In this colossal format, the head of Pierre de Wissant – one of the six members of the town council who offered themselves as sacrifices in order to save the city of Calais – has a greater intensity of expression and inner emotion, relieved of any illustrative function. There is no longer any evidence of this sculpture's association with the design for the monument. Through fragments of figures like this, Rodin laid the basis for the subjectivism of sculpture in the modern period. It is possible that the actor Coquelin Cadet, a member of the ensemble of the Comédie française, was Rodin's model for the figure of Pierre de Wissant.[1]

After Georg Treu saw the work in Berlin in 1909, he wrote enthusiastically to Rodin: "I have just seen the colossal head which is at the Royal Academy in Berlin. In its expressiveness and in its size, it is a truly gripping work of art! Could I have the cast for the Albertinum? And for what price? I would be happy to be able to exhibit it with your other works in the collection."[2] Just a few days later, Treu wrote to the Academy that Rodin in-

tended to give the head to the Skulpturensammlung as a gift as soon as the exhibition was over.

As an archaeologist, Georg Treu would have had a special feel for this colossal sculpture, and this may be the reason why he was so keen to acquire it. After all, the painful expression on the face of Pierre de Wissant is reminiscent of works of Hellenistic sculpture, such as the group depicting "Laocoon" and his sons (Rome, Vatican Museums). The representation of mental states, emotions and human suffering was the crucial innovation of the art of that period, along with the precise observation of physical movement and the body's musculature. Perhaps, in turn, it was the art of classical antiquity, with its sometimes colossal fragments, that inspired Rodin to create this enlargement.[3]

1 Elsen 2003, Cat. no. 31, p. 141 f.
2 Treu to Rodin on 1 February 1909 (transcript), Archive of the Skulpturensammlung, Staatliche Kunstsammlungen Dresden, Artist file Rodin I.
3 Exh. cat. Berlin 1979, p. 139.

Gustav Mahler

1909

The Austrian composer and conductor Gustav Mahler (1860–1911) first attracted attention as conductor of the German Opera in Prague. This was followed by sojourns in Leipzig, at the opera houses in Budapest, at the Stadttheater in Hamburg and at the Vienna Hofoper. In 1908 he took up his position at the Metropolitan Opera in New York. Mahler was not only one of the greatest composers of his era, but was also regarded as one of the best conductors, and he reformed contemporary musical theatre by introducing important innovations.

This bronze portrait of Gustav Mahler was shown in Dresden for the first time at the 1912 Great Art Exhibition. However, it was not the painter Gotthardt Kuehl, as the responsible exhibition director, who sought to acquire the portrait for Dresden – it was Georg Treu, who had already contacted Rodin to request the work for the collection in the Albertinum. A fascinating story developed surrounding its acquisition, which only became possible through Treu using his personal influence to obtain the necessary funds. In a letter to one of the potential donors, Consul General Von Klemperer, the director of the Dresdner Bank, he wrote: "At the Great Art Exhibition in this city, there is a bronze bust of the composer Mahler by Rodin, in my opinion one of the most excellent portraits ever produced by this great sculptor. […] The purchase of this work by Rodin is all the more to be recommended in view of the fact that Rodin is now in his 72nd year and so it is important to hurry in order to secure something by him."[1] Treu succeeded in persuading his financier, with whom he had come into contact via Woldemar von Seidlitz and who had originally wished

to invest in a collection of antique vitreous enamel objects for the Museum, with the result that the purchase was made in June 1912.

Recalling the time when Mahler was sitting for his portrait after returning from New York, Alma Mahler said: "I watched Rodin with fascination for fourteen days as he worked. […] He never took anything away with the palette knife but added tiny little balls, and in the breaks between the sittings, he smoothed the new bumps."[2]

The portrait evokes particular fascination through the association of music and art. The composer and conductor is represented with his head held high and with an almost meditative bearing, his gaze extending into the distance as if he were immersed in the sound of music. A nervous tension in Mahler, which was confirmed by his widow, is clearly evident in the asymmetrical facial features and the eyes, which have a sketchy appearance and are each modelled differently. Although in this portrait Rodin reproduced the features of Mahler, creating a clear physiognomic likeness, he toyed with double and multiple meanings – as he frequently did in his works – by giving a later marble version of this sculpture (1910/11) the title "Mozart", thus calling the individuality of the subject into question.

1 Treu to Von Klemperer, 31 May 1912 (transcript), Archive of the Skulpturensammlung, Staatliche Kunstsammlungen Dresden, Artist file Rodin I.
2 Alma Mahler-Werfel, Erinnerungen an Gustav Mahler, Frankfurt am Main/Berlin/Wien 1971, p. 178.

Triton and Nereid

c. 1886–1893 (design); posthumous cast

This bronze is evidently an unauthorised cast after the terracotta model held in the Metropolitan Museum of Art in New York, which is closely related in form to Rodin's "Minotaur" (c. 1886).[1] The work is also known under other titles, the artist himself preferred "The Minotaur", referring to the myth of Minos and Pasiphae. After her union with a bull, Pasiphae gave birth to the Minotaur, to whom the Athenians had to sacrifice seven maidens and seven youths each year, until the monster was eventually killed by Theseus.[2] Nevertheless, Rodin emphasised that what is important in this group is not so much the theme itself but rather the life-like modelling of the muscles.[3] In this fragmental group, Rodin has turned "The Minotaur" into a highly erotic composition. Two mythological creatures are entwined in a caress. Triton, a son of Poseidon and Amphitrite, embraces his playmate, the sea nymph Nereid, around her waist, pulling her towards himself and placing a kiss on her back. Rodin clearly took Mannerist and Baroque sculptural groups on the theme of abduction as the inspiration for this work.

Half a dozen bronze casts of this work are known. These are held in Leipzig (Museum der bildenden Künste),[4] Glauchau (Museum und Kunstsammlung Schloss Hinterglauchau), Marburg (private collection, previously Chemnitz) and Wellesley, USA (Davis Museum, Wellesley College) as well as one further cast without a base in a private collection.[5] During Rodin's lifetime, these bronzes did not yet exist, and even the Musée Rodin in Paris does not have a plaster version among its holdings.[6] Thus, it can be assumed that Rodin did not make a plaster cast from the terracotta model, lending it the status of a unique specimen. As early as 1979 Claude Keisch expressed his suspicion that the bronzes were produced without authorisation, and in an expert's report drawn up in 2000 even Schmoll gen. Eisenwerth, proceeded from the assumption that after the purchase of the terracotta original in New York (1912) and before the earliest purchase of the bronze (1956 in Leipzig) a plaster cast must have been produced from which the unauthorised bronze casts were created.[7] These bronzes differ from the casts produced in limited numbers at the Musée Rodin in that the works in this series are not stamped and dated, indicating that they were produced posthumously. Furthermore, they are not based on an original plaster model by the artist but on the new plaster model moulded from the terracotta.

1 "Faun and Nymphe", "Jupiter Taurus", Tancock 1976, pp. 270–273. Inv. no. of the terracotta model 12.11.2, purchased 1912.
2 Brewer's Concise Dictionary of Phrase and Fable, Oxford, 1992, p. 676.
3 Gsell 1979, p. 157.
4 Herwig Guratzsch, Museum der bildenden Künste Leipzig, Katalog der Bildwerke, Cologne 1999, p. 275.
5 Archive of the Skulpturensammlung, Staatliche Kunstsammlungen Dresden, Artist file Rodin II. Information kindly provided by Alicia LaTores, Davis Museum at Wellesley College.
6 A larger-scale plaster does exist however (Inv. no. p. 5687), cf. Rodin. La lumière de l'antique, Exh. cat. Arles/Paris, Paris 2013. Information kindly provided by Chloé Ariot, Musée Rodin.
7 Exh. cat. Berlin 1979, p. 120, Cat. no. 22; Archive of the Skulpturensammlung, Staatliche Kunstsammlungen Dresden, Artist file Rodin II. See also Tancock 1976, p. 273.

List

Man with the Broken Nose
1863/64
Bronze, 31.5 × 19.5 × 15.5 cm
(base: 7.8 × 13 × 13 cm)
Signed in front below the neck: Rodin
Albertinum/Skulpturensammlung, Inv.
ZV 1288. Purchased from the artist, 1894.

The Age of Bronze
1877
Plaster, 181 × 66 × 70 cm
Signed at top of base: Rodin
Albertinum/Skulpturensammlung,
Inv. Abg.-ZV 1885 (ASN 1738).
Purchased from the artist, 1894.

Saint John the Baptist
1878
Plaster, 201.5 × 85 × 127 cm
Signed on base in front of the right foot:
A. Rodin
Albertinum/Skulpturensammlung,
Abg.-ZV 2480 (ASN 4806).
Purchased at the International Art
Exhibition, Dresden, 1901. Donated by
a private citizen (Karl August Lingner).
Inventoried in 1902.

Eve
c. 1881
Marble (before 1900), 78 × 26 × 33 cm
Signed on the back: A. Rodin
Albertinum/Skulpturensammlung,
Inv. ZV 1890. Purchased from the artist
at the World's Fair in Paris. Inventoried
in 1901.

Small male torso (»Torse de Giganti«)
1880s
Bronze, 27.3 × 18.6 × 11.3 cm
Signed on right side below: Rodin
Albertinum/Skulpturensammlung,
Inv. ZV 1737. Purchased from Geh.
Regierungsrat Woldemar von Seidlitz at
the 1st International Art Exhibition in
Dresden in 1897 and donated to the
Skulpturensammlung.

Jean Paul Laurens
1882
Bronze (1896–1900), 58 × 38.5 × 31.5 cm
Signed at bottom of right shoulder:
A. Rodin; Foundry mark low down on back:
L. Perzinka/Fondeur/Versailles
Albertinum/Skulpturensammlung,
Inv. ZV 1888. Purchased from the artist
at the World's Fair in Paris. Inventoried
in 1901.

Jean d'Aire (The Man with the Key)
1886/1887
Plaster, 205 × 67.5 × 63.5 cm
Albertinum/Skulpturensammlung,
Inv. Abg.-ZV 2481 (ASN 4804). Purchased
at the International Art Exhibition, Dresden,
1901. Donated by Theodor and Erwin
Bienert, Dresden. Inventoried 1902.

Crying Danaid
c. 1889
Plaster, 28 × 19 × 24 cm
Albertinum/Skulpturensammlung,
Inv. Abg.-ZV 2645 (ASN 4811). Donated
by the artist, 1904.

Pierre Puvis de Chavannes
1891
Plaster, 56 × 51 × 29.5 cm
Albertinum/Skulpturensammlung,
Inv. Abg.-ZV 2538 (ASN 4812).
Purchased at the International Art Exhibi-
tion, Dresden, 1901. Donated by Louis
Uhle, Dresden. Inventoried 1902.

**Victor Hugo, »Heroic Bust«,
first version**
1896
Plaster, 73.5 × 59 × 57 cm
Albertinum/Skulpturensammlung,
Inv. ZV 1719 (ASN 4815). Purchased
at the 1st International Art Exhibition,
Dresden, 1897.

The Inner Voice
1896
Plaster, 149.5 × 70 × 60 cm
Albertinum/Skulpturensammlung,
Inv. Abg.-ZV 2070 (ASN 4816).
Purchased at the 1st International Art
Exhibition, Dresden, 1897.

Jean d'Aire (The Man with the Key)
1884/86 (design), c. 1884–1899
(execution/reduced-scale cast)
Bronze, 47 × 16.3 × 14.5 cm
Signed on robe on back behind the
right foot: Rodin; Foundry mark on back:
L. Perzinka/Fondeur
Albertinum/Skulpturensammlung,
Inv. ZV 1889. Purchased from the artist
at the World Exhibition in Paris. Inventoried
in 1901.

Alexandre Falguière
1899
Plaster, 43 × 24 × 25 cm
Signed: Rodin
Albertinum/Skulpturensammlung,
Inv. Abg.-ZV 2628 (ASN 1569). Donated
by the artist, 1904.

The Thinker
1903
(Colossal version; the figure for the
tympanum of the »Gates of Hell« was
created in the early 1880s, the enlarged
version in 1903)
Plaster, 183.5 × 102.5 × 149 cm
Albertinum/Skulpturensammlung,
Inv. Abg.-ZV 2627 (ASN 4817).
Purchased at the Art Exhibition, Dresden,
1904; donated by a private citizen
(Fritz Emil Günther).

Eugène Guillaume
1903
Plaster, 39 × 32 × 28 cm
Albertinum/Skulpturensammlung,
Inv. Abg.-ZV 2629 (ASN 1025).
Donated by the artist, 1904.

Colossal head of Pierre de Wissant
1909
Plaster, 83 × 48 × 55 cm
Signed on base below right ear: A. Rodin
Albertinum/Skulpturensammlung,
Inv. Abg.-ZV 2951 (ASN 4805).
Donated by the artist, 1909.

Gustav Mahler
1909
Bronze, 33 × 24.5 × 25.5 cm
(base: 12.3 × 15 × 15 cm)
Signed on left: A. Rodin; Stamp inside:
A. Rodin; Foundry mark on back of neck:
ALEXiS RUDiER/FONDEUR PARIS,
below: M
Albertinum/Skulpturensammlung,
Inv. ZV 2488. Purchased at the Great Art
Exhibiton, Dresden, 1912. Donated by Von
Klemperer and Dr. Naumann, Dresden.

Triton and Nereid
c. 1886 – 1893 (design); posthumous cast
Bronze, 36.8 × 23.5 × 19.5 cm (base:
6.8 × 15 × 15 cm)
Signed under left thigh of the Nereid:
A. Rodin; on left cut-off knee of the
Nereid: AR
Albertinum/Skulpturensammlung,
Inv. ZV 3695. Purchased 1966.

Works missing since 1945:

Paolo and Francesca
Before 1886
Plaster, probably 27 × 57 × 22 cm
Albertinum/Skulpturensammlung,
Inv. Abg.-ZV 2537. Purchased at the
International Art Exhibition, Dresden,
1901. Donated by Louis Uhle, Dresden.
Inventoried 1902.

The Crouching Woman
c. 1882
Plaster, height 32 cm
Albertinum/Skulpturensammlung,
Inv. Abg.-ZV 2644. Donated by the artist,
1904.

Small group of two female fauns
(according to list of casts entering
the collection; probably means "three"
female fauns)
c. 1882
Plaster, height 15.5 cm
Albertinum/Skulpturensammlung,
Inv. Abg.-ZV 2646. Donated by the artist,
1904.

Biography

COMPILED BY ELENA RIEGER

1840 Rodin born in Paris on 12 November.

1854–1857 Pupil of Horace Lecoq de Boisbaudran at the Petite École.

1857–1859 Applies three times for admission to the Sculpture department of the "École des Beaux-Arts" (Grand École), each time without success.

1858 Rodin works for several years producing architectural embellishments as part of the urban renewal programme commissioned by Napoleon III.

1860 Rodin produces his first known work: the bust of his father "Jean-Baptiste Rodin".

1862/63 Following the early death of his sister Maria, Rodin joins a Catholic order, the "Pères du Très-Saint-Sacrement" (Congregation of the Blessed Sacrament) as a novice. After a few months he returns to Paris, where he establishes his own studio in a stable in the rue de la Reine Blanche.

1864 Evening courses with Antoine-Louis Barye and work in the sculpture studio of Albert-Ernest Carrier-Belleuse. Rodin meets Rose Beuret, with whom he lives for the rest of his life.

1865 The artist attempts to make his debut in the Paris Salon, the annual state art exhibition, submitting the mask of the "Man with the Broken Nose", but it is rejected.

1866 Birth of his son Auguste-Eugène Beuret.

1870 Conscription into the National Guard during the Franco-Prussian War; discharged early.

1871 First participation in an exhibition in Brussels and renewed collaboration with Carrier-Belleuse, designing ornamentation and architectural embellishments until 1872; transfer to the workshop of Antoine-Joseph van Rasbourgh in 1873.

1875 The marble version of the "Man with the Broken Nose" is the first work by Rodin to be admitted to the Paris Salon.

1876 Travels to Italy (Rome and Florence), where he studies the works of Michelangelo and Donatello; after returning to Brussels, he begins work on "The Age of Bronze".

1877 Exhibition of "The Age of Bronze" in Brussels, then at the Salon in Paris. The artist is accused of having made the statue by casting a living model; Rodin returns to Paris.

1878 Preliminary studies for "Saint John the Baptist"; production of "The Walking Man".

1879 Work at the Sèvres porcelain factory.

1880 Thanks to support from friends in the artistic community, "The Age of Bronze" (in bronze) and "Saint John the Baptist" (in plaster) are exhibited at the Salon and purchased by the French state. Rodin is awarded a government commission to create a portal for the planned

Musée des Arts Décoratifs; Rodin designs the "Gates of Hell", on which he continues to work for the rest of his life. He moves into his studio in the "Dépôt des marbres" in the rue de l'Université.

1881 "Eve", "The Thinker" and the bust of "Jean Paul Laurens" are created; the bronze "Saint John the Baptist" is purchased by the French state after the Salon exhibition.

1882 Creation of busts depicting artist friends, work on the "Ugolino" group.

1883 Further portrait sculptures are produced; Rodin meets the 19-year-old Camille Claudel, who becomes his model, pupil, colleague and lover.

1885 Rodin is commissioned by the City of Calais to design the monument "Burghers of Calais".

1886 Completion of the "Burghers of Calais", presentation of individual works from the "Gates of Hell" in the Galerie Georges Petit in Paris, and commissions from the City of Santiago de Chile for monuments to Benjamín Vicuña Mackenna and General Lynch.

1887 Drawings for Charles Baudelaire's "Flowers of Evil".

1888 Commission from the French state to produce a marble version of "The Kiss" for the 1889 World's Fair; Rodin rents a joint studio with Camille Claudel.

1889 Appointment to the jury of the World's Fair and the Salon; the exhibition of 36 works in the Galerie Georges Petit along with paintings by Claude Monet brings about Rodin's breakthrough; commission for a monument to Claude Lorrain in Nancy and for a monument in honour of Victor Hugo in Paris.

1890 Co-founder of the Société nationale des Beaux-Arts, which consciously deviates from the rules of the state Salon. Rejection of the design for the monument to Victor Hugo.

1891 Commission for a monument to Honoré de Balzac and start of a new design for the monument to Victor Hugo. Rodin travels with Camille Claudel to the Touraine region and visits the Channel Islands.

1893 Rodin succeeds Jules Dalou as Vice-President of the Société nationale des Beaux-Arts.

1894 Commission for a monument to Sarmiento in Buenos Aires, invitation from Claude Monet to Giverny and meeting with Paul Cézanne.

1895 Purchase of the "Villa des Brillants" in Meudon, criticism of the Balzac monument and unveiling of the "Monument to the Burghers of Calais" in Calais.

1897 Rodin is represented by six sculptures at the 1st International Art Exhibition in Dresden, the monument to Victor Hugo is exhibited at the Société nationale des Beaux-Arts.

1898 Final separation from Camille Claudel, the Societé des gens des lettres rejects the design for the Balzac monument after it is exhibited at the Salon.

1899 Commission for a monument to Puvis de Chavannes, the bust of Falguières is created.

1900 First retrospective exhibition featuring 150 works as part of the World's Fair in Paris, presented in a specially built pavilion on the Place de l'Alma; this brings about Rodin's international breakthrough. Rodin becomes a member of the Royal Academy of Fine Arts in Dresden and a corresponding member of the Berlin Secession.

1901 An exhibition featuring photographs of works by Rodin taken by Eugène Druet is shown in the "Galerie des artistes modernes" in Paris, the exhibition pavilion on the Place de l'Alma is dismantled and reconstructed as a studio in Meudon.

1902 Rodin becomes acquainted with Rainer Maria Rilke. Alexis Rudier becomes Rodin's primary caster, a major exhibition opens in Prague.

1903 Appointment as President of the "International Society of Painters, Sculptors and Engravers" in London. Rilke publishes his book "Auguste Rodin".

1904 Presentation of a large plaster version of "The Thinker" in London and a bronze version in Paris, participation in exhibitions in several German cities (Weimar, Krefeld, Leipzig, Düsseldorf, Dresden).

1905 Honorary doctorate awarded by the University of Jena, Rilke becomes Rodin's secretary.

1906 Rilke is dismissed by Rodin, the monumental version of "The Thinker" is erected in front of the Panthéon in Paris and Rodin is appointed a full member of the Academy of Arts in Berlin. The exhibition of his drawings in the Grand-Ducal Museum of Art and Crafts in Weimar provokes a scandal, resulting in the resignation of the museum's director, Harry Graf Kessler.

1907 Reconciliation with Rilke, first comprehensive exhibition of drawings at the "Galerie Bernheim-Jeune" in Paris and award of an honorary doctorate by the University of Glasgow.

1908 Moves into the Hôtel Biron as an urban residence thanks to mediation by Rilke.

Bibliography

1909 The monument to Victor Hugo is set up in the grounds of the Palais Royal.

1910 Appointment as a "Grand Officier" of the Legion of Honour.

1911 After an exhibition at the Academy of Arts in Berlin, Kaiser Wilhelm II refuses to award the Order of Merit to Rodin.

1912 First stroke. Rodin exhibition in Tokyo and opening of a Rodin Room in the Metropolitan Museum in New York.

1913 Rodin travels to.

1914 Publication of "Cathedrals of France" and deterioration of Rodin's state of health. The artist travels to England with Rose Beuret and Judith Cladel, where he donates 18 sculptures to the Victoria and Albert Museum; journey to Rome.

1915 Another journey to Rome and production of the portrait of Pope Benedict XV.

1916 Rodin suffers two further strokes. The artist offers to donate his works to the French state for a Rodin Museum, to be installed in the Hôtel Biron. The Museum opens in 1919.

1917 On 29 January Rodin marries Rose Beuret, who dies shortly afterwards. Rodin dies on 17 November. The artist is buried next to his wife in the park of the Villa des Brillants in Meudon. A statue of "The Thinker" is erected above the grave.

Exh. cat. Berlin 1979
Rodin. Plastik, Zeichnungen, Graphik, Ausst.-Kat. Staatliche Museen zu Berlin, Alte Nationalgalerie, Berlin 1979, Claude Keisch (ed.), Berlin 1979.

Exh. cat. Dresden 1994
Das Albertinum vor 100 Jahren – Die Skulpturensammlung Georg Treus, Exh. cat. Skulpturensammlung, Staatliche Kunstsammlungen Dresden, Albertinum, Dresden 1994, Kordelia Knoll (ed.), Dresden 1994.

Exh. cat. Hamburg/Dresden 2006
Vor 100 Jahren. Rodin in Deutschland, Exh. cat. Bucerius Kunst Forum Hamburg/ Skulpturensammlung, Staatliche Kunstsammlungen Dresden 2006, Ortrud Westheider, Heinz Spielmann, Astrid Nielsen, Moritz Woelk (eds.), München 2006.

Exh. cat. Marl 1997
Auguste Renoir. Die Bürger von Calais – Werk und Wirkung, Exh. cat. Skulpturenmuseum Glaskasten Marl, Marl 1997/1998/ Musée Royal de Mariemont, Morlanwelz 1998, Skulpturenmuseum Glaskasten Marl (ed.), Ostfildern-Ruit 1997.

Exh. cat. Marseille 1997
Rodin. La voix intérieure, Exh. cat. Musée des Beaux Arts de Marseille, Marseille 1997, Luc Georget, Antoinette Le Normand-Romain (ed.), Marseille 1997.

Exh. cat. Paris 2001
Rodin en 1900. L'exposition de l'Alma, Exh. cat. Musée du Luxembourg, Paris 2001.

Exh. cat. Paris 2003
D'ombre et de marbre. Hugo face à Rodin, Exh. cat. Maison de Victor Hugo, Paris 2003/2004, Martine Contensou, Alexandrine Achille (eds.), Paris 2003.

Exh. cat. Paris 2017
Rodin. Le livre du centenaire, Exh. cat. Grand Palais, Galeries nationales, Paris 2017, Catherine Chevillot, Antoinette Le Normand-Romain (eds.), Paris 2017.

Exh. cat. Washington 1981
Rodin Rediscovered, Exh. cat. National Gallery of Art, Washington 1981/1982, Albert E. Elsen (ed.), Washington 1981.

Exh. cat. Wien 2010
Rodin und Wien, Exh. cat. Belvedere Wien, Wien 2010/2011, Agnes Husslein-Arco, Stephan Koja (eds.), München 2010.

Clemen 1905
Paul Clemen, Auguste Rodin, in: Die Kunst für alle 20 (1904/1905), pp. 289–307, pp. 321–335.

Elsen 1965
Albert E. Elsen (Hg.), Auguste Rodin. Readings on His Life and Work, Englewood Cliffs 1965.

Gsell 1979
Paul Gsell (ed.), Auguste Rodin.
Die Kunst. Gespräche des Meisters,
collected by Paul Gsell, Zürich 1979.

Höcherl 2003
Heike Höcherl, Rodins Gipse.
Ursprünge moderner Plastik, Frankfurt
am Main 2003.

Keisch 1979
Claude Keisch, Rodin. Klassiker einer
unklassischen Kunst, in: Dresdener Kunstblätter 6/1979, pp. 162–173.

Keisch 1994
Claude Keisch, Georg Treu und Rodin,
in: Das Albertinum vor 100 Jahren –
Die Skulpturensammlung Georg Treus,
Exh. cat. Staatliche Kunstsammlungen
Dresden, Albertinum, Dresden 1994/1995,
Kordelia Knoll (ed.), Dresden 1994,
pp. 218–224.

Keisch 1998
Claude Keisch, Rodin dans l'Allemagne
de Guillaume II. Partisans et détracteurs
à Leipzig, Dresde et Berlin, Paris 1998.

Le Normand-Romain 2007
Antoinette Le Normand-Romain, Rodin
et le Bronze. Catalogue des œuvres
conservées au Musée Rodin, 2 vols.,
Paris 2007.

Lier 1896/97
Hermann Arthur Lier, Die Internationale
Kunstausstellung in Dresden, in: Kunst-
chronik, N. F. 8 (1896/1897), Heft 32,
pp. 497–504.

Mattiussi 2010
Véronique Mattiussi, Von Mahler bis
Mozart. Geschichte eines Porträts,
in: Rodin und Wien, Exh. cat. Belvedere
Wien, Wien 2010/2011, Agnes
Husslein-Arco, Stephan Koja (eds.),
München 2010.

Nielsen/Woelk 2006
Astrid Nielsen, Moritz Woelk, Rodin
in Dresden. Erbe der Hellenen?
in: Vor 100 Jahren. Rodin in Deutschland,
Exh. cat. Bucerius Kunst Forum Hamburg/
Skulpturensammlung, Staatliche
Kunstsammlungen Dresden 2006,
München 2006, pp. 42–51.

Rilke 1920
Rainer Maria Rilke, Auguste Rodin,
Leipzig 1920.

Schmoll gen. Eisenwerth 1983
Josef Adolph Schmoll gen. Eisenwerth,
Rodin-Studien. Persönlichkeit – Werke –
Wirkung – Bibliographie, München 1983.

Tancock 1976
John L. Tancock, The Sculpture of
Auguste Rodin. The Collection of the
Rodin Museum Philadelphia, Philadelphia
1976.

Treu 1903
Georg Treu, Auguste Rodin, in: Jahrbuch
der bildenden Kunst 2, 1903, pp. 81–86.

Treu 1904/05
Georg Treu, Bei Rodin, in: Kunst und
Künstler 1904/05, pp. 3–17.

Wohlrab 2016
Christiane Wohlrab, Non-finito als Topos
der Moderne. Die Marmorskulpturen von
Auguste Rodin, Paderborn 2016.

Credits

1st edition 2017

© Staatliche Kunstsammlungen Dresden
Skulpturensammlung
and Sandstein Verlag, Dresden

Photo Credits

Albertinum/Skulpturensammlung,
Staatliche Kunstsammlungen Dresden
pp. 4, 7, 9, 10 (Archive Skulpturensammlung), 12 (Archive Skulpturensammlung, Artist file Rodin I), 13
(in: Offizieller Katalog der Internationalen Kunstausstellung, Dresden 1897,
Tafelteil), 14, 15 (in: Dekorative Kunst 4
(1901), vol. 10, pp. 379, 381), 16
(Archive Skulpturensammlung, Artist
file Rodin I), 18, 19, 20, 21 (Archive
Skulpturensammlung, Artist file
Rodin I), 24, 25, 26, 29, 32 (Archive
Skulpturensammlung)

Albertinum/Galerie Neue Meister,
Staatliche Kunstsammlungen Dresden
p. 11

Musée Rodin, Paris
p. 5 (Inv.-Nr. Ph 203), 22

SLUB Dresden/Deutsche Fotothek
pp. 6, 8, 28

David Brandt
p. 30

Jürgen Karpinski
p. 47

Hans-Peter Klut/Elke Estel
pp. 4, 7, 9, 10, 11, 18, 20, 39, 45, 49, 59,
61, 63, 71, 73

Werner Lieberknecht
pp. 37, 41, 43, 51, 53, 55, 57, 65, 67, 69

Copy-editing

Christine Jäger-Ulbricht
Sandstein Verlag

Translation into English

Anglo-Saxon Language Service,
Geradine Schuckelt

Typesetting and reprography

Gudrun Diesel, Jana Neumann
Sandstein Verlag

Layout

Bettina Neustadt
Sandstein Verlag

Printing

FINIDR s.r.o., Český Těšín

www.sandstein-verlag.de
ISBN 978-3-95498-361-2

The Deutsche Nationalbibliothek
holds a record of this publication in the
Deutsche Nationalbibliografie; detailed
bibliographical data can be found
under http://dnb.ddb.de.